# KOSOVO:

## THE SCORE

THE LORD BYRON FOUNDATION FOR BALKAN STUDIES was founded by the late Sir Alfred Sherman in 1994 as a non-partisan research center devoted to studying the Balkan Peninsula in all its aspects. The Foundation's research, publications and conferences are designed to correct the current trend of public commentary, which tends, systematically, not to understand events but to construct a propagandistic version of Balkan rivalries. The Foundation provides a forum and a platform for specialists and commentators who wish to reassert their independence and objectivity. It is named after a great Western poet who gave his life in the fight to free Balkan Christians from Mohammedan rule. This choice reflects its belief in the essential unity of our civilization, of which the Orthodox Christian nations are an inseparable, essential ingredient. The work of The Lord Byron Foundation is based on the acceptance that the cause of tolerance in a troubled region can never be advanced by misrepresentation, by the sentimental lapse of seriousness and by mendacity that all too often characterizes current Western policies in the region.

THE AMERICAN COUNCIL FOR KOSOVO is a U.S. nonprofit organization dedicated to promoting a better understanding of the Serbian province of Kosovo and Metohija and of the critical American stake in the province's future. The Council's mission is to make accurate information and analysis about Kosovo available to officials of the Executive and Legislative branches of the U.S. Government; to think tanks, media, NGOs, religious and advocacy organizations; and to the general public. The Council believes that a reconsideration can and will occur if accurate information and analysis is made available to the American government and people regarding what is at stake in Kosovo and why U.S. policymakers should reject the option of Kosovo independence.

The American Council for Kosovo is an activity of Squire Sanders Public Advocacy, LLC, and Global Strategic Communications Group, which are registered under the Foreign Agents Registration Act as agents for the Serbian National Council of Kosovo and Metohija. Additional information with respect to this matter is on file with the Foreign Agents Registration Unit of the Department of Justice in Washington DC.

# KOSOVO:
## THE SCORE
### 1999-2009

The American Council for Kosovo
The Lord Byron Foundation for Balkan Studies

Washington D.C.-Chicago-Ottawa

Published in the United States by
The American Council for Kosovo and
The Lord Byron Foundation for Balkan Studies
Washington D.C.-Chicago-Ottawa

ISBN 978-1-892478-05-4

# CONTENTS

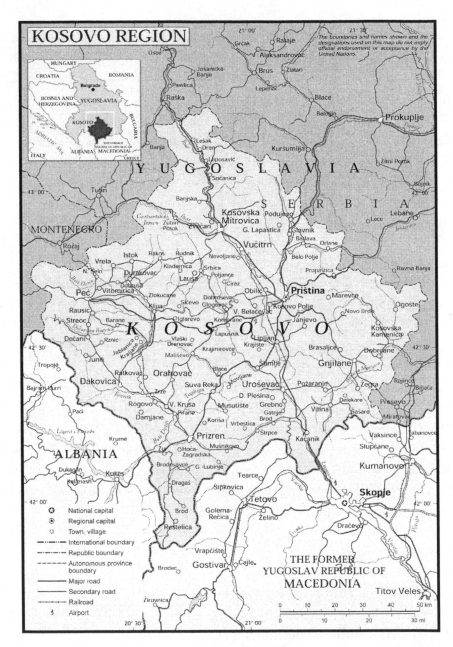

KOSOVO 1999

# Foreword

*James Bissett*[1]

Ten years ago NATO bombed Serbia, illegally and without provocation. The anniversary did not gain much media attention in the West. It was not celebrated by those NATO countries that took part in the war because it was not an episode of which any of them should be proud.

For 78 days and nights the most intensive bombing offensive suffered by any country since the end of the Second World War continued. Thousands of people were killed and the civilian infrastructure of Serbia was destroyed, but the bombing proved unable to degrade the Serbian military. It caused far more suffering than it prevented.

For the first time since its founding the North Atlantic Alliance – led by the United States – acted in violation of its own treaty and the United Nations Charter by using violence to resolve an international dispute. This illegal act marked a historical turning point. It was a fatal step in dismantling the framework of security that had governed international relations since the end of the Second World War. It set precedents that will continue to plague international affairs for years. The bombing also revealed a disturbing reality that has continued to haunt us: the ease with which our democratic countries can be led into committing acts of violence and war by political leaders prepared to tell us lies.

President Clinton, Prime Minister Blair and other NATO leaders told their citizens that the bombing of Serbia was a humanitarian intervention to stop President Milosevic of Serbia from committing genocide and the ethnic cleansing of the Albanian majority in Kosovo. This of course was not true: forensic times have found some

1 Ambassador Bissett is Chairman of The Lord Byron Foundation for Balkan Studies. He was Canadian Ambassador to Yugoslavia (1990 – 1992).

2000 victims of the Kosovo conflict so far – Serbian and Albanian, civilian and military – who had been killed prior to NATO's air war in March 1999. Distressing as this figure may be, it is not genocide. Nevertheless, the accusations that genocide took place in Kosovo continue to be accepted without hesitation by the western media.

The claim about ethnic cleansing was also a falsehood. While it is true that several thousand Albanians had been displaced within Kosovo by the armed conflict between the Serb security forces and the Kosovo Liberation Army (KLA), the large-scale exodus of the Albanian population occurred *after* the bombing started. United Nations figures show that the mass of refugees fled Kosovo after the first bombs began to fall In other words, it was the bombing that caused the flight from Kosovo. Despite the proof of this we continue to hear in the western media that the NATO bombing "stopped ethnic cleansing."

In reality the bombing of Serbia had nothing to do with genocide or ethnic cleansing. The bombing had everything to do with demonstrating that NATO was still a viable military organization and was needed in Europe. There is ample evidence now to show that the United States and British secret services aided and abetted the KLA in its efforts to use violence to destabilize Kosovo and to create the excuse for NATO intervention.

The Kosovo crisis and the 78 day bombing campaign against Serbia was from the outset a carefully planned fraud. Because bombing people for humanitarian reasons was an obvious contradiction, it had to be portrayed as an urgently needed rescue mission to stop the "genocide" that was allegedly taking place in Kosovo. This was done by a highly organized publicity campaign designed to deceive a compliant media and a gullible public that Slobodan Milosevic of Serbia was evil and that the Serbs were barbarians who had to be stopped. Hailed as the man who brought the Bosnian war to a conclusion at Dayton four years earlier, he was now depicted as the "butcher of the Balkans" and conveniently charged by The Hague War Crimes Tribunal as a war criminal. The duplicity and the deception which reached their height during the bombing itself has continued to this day.

This publication is intended to commemorate the tenth anniversary of the NATO bombing by supplying the missing pieces in the Kosovo puzzle. It reveals how subsequent policies followed by the United States and its NATO allies have not only continued to be based on falsehood and hypocrisy but also pose a threat to world peace and security.

The contributing writers are experts who were not deceived by NATO's "humanitarian intervention" and were appalled at the ease with which our political leaders were prepared to violate principles underpinning the very essence of western civilization – such as territorial integrity, sovereignty, and the rule of law.

The heart of the problem has been what appears to be a determination of the United States policy makers, whether Democrat or Republican, to look upon the Western Balkans as their special fiefdom where international rules of conduct do not apply. It is as if they regard these Slavic lands as lesser breeds without the law, and therefore can do with them whatever they deem desirable. This hubris has lead the United States and the obedient but morally bankrupt leaders of Germany, France and Great Britain to follow wrong-headed policies such as the bombing of Serbia and the recognition of Kosovo independence – and to do so without scruples.

Perhaps it is too much to hope for that the critical financial problems faced by the United States and many European countries will curtail their meddling in the affairs of smaller nations and give them pause to reflect that the rule of law applies to all and that international disputes must be resolved without the use of force. This is the hope – however tenuous - expressed by the contributors to this volume on the tenth anniversary of the bombing of Serbia.

# Kosovo and the American Century

*Sir Alfred Sherman*[1]

The American century began with the Spanish-American War, whose effects are still with us. It ended in 1999 with American penetration of the Balkans and bombing of Serbia.

The Spanish-American war, besides expressing "manifest destiny," was designed to oust Spain from its last footholds in the New World and strengthen the US's strategic position in the Gulf of Mexico, the Caribbean and Pacific.

By contrast, U.S. intervention in the Balkans has no rational strategic aim. It is allegedly an ongoing incursion on behalf of the "international community," supposedly justified by the "evolving" concepts of international jurisprudence (e.g. "humanitarian intervention"). Its tangible fruits include a Jihadist stronghold in Bosnia and the dynamics of a Greater Albania, which paves the way for further wars. Far from creating a new status quo it has simply intensified instability. The U.S. may succeed in establishing its hegemony in the Balkans-Danubia-Carpathia, but it will also inherit long-standing ethno-religious conflicts and border disputes without the means for settling them.

SERBOPHOBIA AND WESTERN SELF-HATRED – Not for the first time, the Serbs are being subjected to a pogrom. As in the case of all pogroms, the cause

---

1  Sir Alfred Sherman (1919-2006), writer, journalist, political analyst and former advisor to Prime Minister Margaret Thatcher, was a co-founder and – until March 2001 – Chairman of The Lord Byron Foundation for Balkan Studies. This is Sir Alfred's final paper on the Balkans, written shortly before his death in August 2006. He presented it in an abbreviated form at a symposium on Kosovo at the Serbian Academy of Sciences and Arts in Belgrade in March 2006. This is the first time it is published in full.

lies in the nature of the perpetrators, not the victim's. The West, that is to say NATO, which has been leading the pogrom, is beset by deep distemper, one of whose many manifestations has been chronic Serbophobia. This is one symptom of the ingrained masochism and national or civilizational self-hatred which has been plaguing the West increasingly since the dawn of the last century.

The self-hatred has taken many forms. *Nostalgie de la boue*, emotional identification with backward societies, blind sympathy with destructive revolutionary forces and regimes, and crude Islamophilia are among the symptoms. It is mainly a product of the twentieth century, though antecedents can be traced earlier. Communism exemplifies it. Magical wisdom and powers were accorded to the proletariat, flying in the face of logic and experience. The conceited claims of semi-literate monsters like Stalin and Mao were taken at face value, their assaults on civilization assisted. In many parts of Britain, Christian symbols and practices are outlawed or hindered by authorities on the grounds that they constitute discrimination against non-Christian minorities.

Similar action is taken against literary and historical expressions of Britishness. Britain is beginning to feel like an occupied country. As a result, associated cardinal values: patriotism, loyalty, the family, morality are under threat. In her years as leader of the Opposition and then prime minister, Margaret Thatcher met opposition from her colleagues and the media to her enunciating a Christian view on socio-political affairs.

Christianity continually needs creative restatement in light of science and social change. The exploitation of patriotism by fascism in its various forms has left national values exposed. The moral and intellectual vacuum generated by the decline of national consciousness, patriotism and Christianity has opened the way for worship of strange Gods. Among them, Islam, the world of the Near East, beckons.

Reality is not far behind ideas. Europe, which for centuries was the source of migration, peopling the Americas, Oceania and parts of Africa, has become the target for mass immigration by Islam, Asia and Africa. The immigrants have set up their own states within a state, and are readily granted privileges to enable them to recreate their *milieux*. Much of social and economic policy is designed to favor them and maintain their separate identity. By now, Moslems have breached the ten per cent barrier in several countries of Western and Central Europe. Governments seem helpless or unwilling to stem the tide. Spokesmen for the European Union laud this Moslem colonization as Europe and the Islamic world as coming together, ignoring its utter one-sidedness.

Criticism of these trends is stifled as "racism", ignoring considerations of patriotism, national consciousness and social order. The undermining of national homogeneity based on common values is leading to visible social breakdown. In whole areas of London, the English are in a minority. Communal cohesion has suffered as a result. Man still does not live by bread alone, but the refurbishment of spiritual values may not be an autonomous process. Emigration by Europeans, particularly to North America, is increasing while the third world, mainly Moslems, rushes in to take their place. Public spiritedness, once based on commonality of national sentiment, is correspondingly declining.

These developments are reflected in policy. In dealing with former Yugoslavia, it is taken for granted by policy-makers and commentators that so-called *Bosniaks*, a product of Ottoman rule, are the indigenous population and are oppressed by alien Serbs. Ignorance of Balkan history facilitates this distortion, but underlying it is alienation from a sense of Euro-Christian history and values. It is no accident that the United States has been leading this gadarene rush. Sense of history is not America's strong point. Immigrants came to shake the dust of imperial Europe off their feet, but in fact transplanted it. The tone-setters: academics; communicators; entertainers, and politicians; are boring away at America's entrails.

Serbdom is particularly vulnerable to these trends. During the Second World War, the British colluded with the Soviets in imposing a communist dictatorship on Yugoslavia. The interests of the long-suffering Serb nation were subordinated to Tito's megalomaniac designs, which included harnessing the Moslem world to Soviet cold-war expansionism while Communist Yugoslavia gained additional status as a major Soviet partner.

*Pace* Karl Marx, most human history (and much of pre-history) is the history of religion. Only during the twentieth century, and particularly its closing stages, has massive de-Christianization been occurring, almost unremarked, its crucial importance ignored. Concurrent Western Islamophilia, both in its rhetoric and, more importantly, implicit in its policy, is just one outcome of this massive historic evolution.

For the Serb nation, this process has been immediately calamitous. In the longer run the West is likely to suffer from the process, as was the case of the First World War, but the Serbs are paying the price now. We should never forget that the anti-Slav, pro-Moslem policies of the Western nations brought about a state of affairs in which Germany felt strong enough to launch the Great War in 1914, which did such serious damage to our civilization.

The Euro-American pogrom against the Serbs totally ignores their beleaguered Christian essence and traditions. This can be put down in part to the West's compulsive secularization, in part to the Serbs' own long integration into Yugoslavia and particularly the communist period, and in part to aping of Western secularism.

Religion and religious affairs have largely vanished from the Western political agenda. By contrast, Marxism and other socialist fallacies seem to have survived the socialist world's collapse, and dominate contemporary Western social thinking more than ever. The ruling ideology is vulgar-Marxist and "optimistic," in its refusal to see the dark side of life. The belief in a quick fix eclipses all.

THE ROLE OF ISLAM –While the West undergoes de-Christianization, Islam is resurgent. Between 1800 and 1950 almost all Moslem polities came under Christian rule, but there was no effort to Christianize them. By now over fifty Moslem sates exist, and many are rich thanks to oil and gas. Moslems migrate from their own failed societies to the West, where they create a hard core. Though in Britain they account for fewer than five percent of the population, mosque attendance is said to outstrip church attendance.

Opinions differ over the cause of the continued hold Islam has over its adherents in the future. There are no grounds for expecting change of any meaningful magnitude within foreseeable time-scales. Perhaps Islam is protected from change by the backwardness of its societies, which it institutionalizes and perpetuates.

More important for us is the attitude prevailing in the West to Islam. In its simplest form it constitutes appeasement, defeatism and sycophancy. In the name of liberality, tolerance, anti-discrimination, and other "multicultural" virtues, the Western political classes manifest the moral, intellectual and political cowardice that seems to have become their hallmark. In Britain, mass immigration of Third World Moslems was permitted without the slightest discussion of its consequences. All questioning has been outlawed as 'racism,' in defiance of logic and common sense. Hence, in regard to former Yugoslavia, the side of the Moslems was taken against the Serbs without any thought as to meaning or history.

It is customary to talk about "The Serbs" when we trace reactions to Tito. But the Serbs had ceased to be a coherent entity long before 1974. Some Serbs were communists. Some were Yugoslavists. Christian Serbia has lacked a political voice. At its time of greatest trial, in the past decade, it lacked political leadership. Contemporaneously, there has been no one to rally Christians in the wider world to their duty in the Balkans.

This is a measure of the crisis affecting Serbia, Christian Serbia, and the wider Christian world. It will need to be grappled with *inside the Christian framework*, within the two millennia of combined spiritual and secular history.

Those of us who draw attention to the Moslem dimension in the Yugoslav crisis are often accused of seeking to launch "a new crusade." Nothing could be further from the truth. Coexistence with the Moslem world is essential, like coexistence among Christians and among Moslems, where most conflict has taken place, and will continue to do so. But this is possible only on the basis of truth. We are entering a new phase in Islam's relations with what we call for want of a better word 'the West', which began half a century ago. We have been reluctant to come to terms with it, but it will be with us for decades to come.

The essence of the change was fourfold.

First, the liberation of the Muslim world from Western rule and domination; secondly, the Muslim world's response with a new, or rather renewed, Islamic militancy; thirdly, concurrently an increase in what Orwell called the West's "negative nationalism" – masochistic self-hatred in Western self-image and policy-making; and lastly, a linked tendency to collective self-deception in relation to Islam. This self-deception encouraged policy-makers and opinion-formers to ignore the gravity of the problem for decades. It is now at work identifying the malaise exclusively with Bin Laden and al Qaeda, whereas they are merely symptoms of a much deeper and more widespread malaise affecting Islam worldwide.

At the end of the First World War almost the whole of the Muslim world was under Western rule. Under that rule they made some progress. Their identity was seen primarily as colonial, and their destiny liberation. In the 60 years that followed, they have enjoyed almost universal liberation from non-Muslim rule. But there is no happy ending. Muslim countries have failed by their own criteria. The shadow of Muslim fundamentalism looms. Country after country eschews elections because they would let in the fundamentalists committed to full sharia and jihad, and outlawing democracy for ever. Muslim countries lack mechanisms for evolution, peaceful constitutional and political change.

In spite of the vast increase in oil wealth, which Muslims believe was placed there by Allah for their particular benefit, there is no commensurate wellbeing, but rather the opposite. Rapid population growth, facilitated by improved medical services, brought population expansion unmatched by resources or employment. The demographic balance has changed, with many more young people lacking regular employment and becoming prey to religious demagogy. Islam's message is beguilingly simple – Muslim solidarity, the Prophet's laws and nothing else, hatred and suspicion of the infidel, paranoia.

This is nothing new. For several centuries, the Muslim world has chosen its religious vocation over scientific and economic progress. In world-historical terms this is the norm, and 'the West' is an exception. We optimistically took for granted that the

Third World would follow in the West's footsteps, but must revise our assumptions. Islam and 'the West' have been increasingly moving in opposite directions and there is every reason for this to continue. There are no major forces for change visible in the Muslim world. "The West," by contrast, is materialistic and liberal in a manner which would have shocked earlier generations.

For centuries, Islam advanced by conquest as well as conversion. When it fell under foreign rule there was no backsliding. Its economic failures have paradoxically expanded it by mass migration, an issue with which Western societies have so far lacked the nerve to grapple - hence the growing, indigestible colonies in Christian heartlands, fifth columns feted and privileged. Civilizations survive or fail thanks to their inner strength of purpose. The question of the day is what Western civilization stands for.

AMERICA'S BALKAN WAR – The Western intervention in the Balkans was America's creation in every sense of the word. How Washington did so is common knowledge. Why it did so, and the implications for American defense and foreign policy generally remain to be elucidated.

During the years that followed, America pulled the strings from the background, and finally intervened openly, on the Moslem side. The most powerful country on earth got deeply involved in Balkan affairs which bear absolutely no relationship to American security. The Kosovo war has been used to "prove" that the demise of the Soviet threat is no reason for phasing out NATO, but on the contrary increasing its role in new areas and new kinds of missions; in other words, NATO is to be an instrument of American policy, whatever that policy might be... and wherever it may be pursued, from Kosovo to Kandahar.

It is hard to hypothesize the basis of US world policy, political, military and economic. Yes, what occurs in the Caribbean Basin is more immediately relevant than the East Asian mainland. One can understand the principle of US involvement in Cuba and Haiti, even though one need not necessarily approve of the particular policies. And yes, America has traditionally been involved in "North Atlantic", i.e., European, affairs, to the extent of two world wars and the Cold War. But what is the relevance of the Balkans and Black Sea? And what is the point of creating and arming militantly Moslem polities in the Balkans?

The US has traditionally worked with some ugly despotisms, and is still doing, so, viz. Saudi Arabia and Kuwait, various Latin-American regimes considered a lesser evil, various unpleasant regimes in Asia, including Pakistan. In any case, democracy cannot be imposed. There are occasions when democracies can be given a helping hand, and others when intervention is counter-productive. But to intervene in favor of Islamic fundamentalism (Bosnia) and barbarity (Kosovo), to help expel Serbs from land they have inhabited as majorities for centuries, does not make sense, unless it was meant to appease the Muslim world.

But then came 9-11, the exercise in freelance Muslim terrorism against a country which has recently done more to extend Muslim rule at the expense of Christian neighbors than any since Palmerston and Disraeli. In retrospect, the act of terror will be seen as a sideshow, and probably a counter-productive irritant, while the problems generated by the USA's quest for hegemony remain to be confronted.

The term *imperialism,* once positive, now pejorative, should be used neutrally. Empires have played a major part in human history, bringing languages, alphabets, religions, communications, culture and government. The Greek, Roman, Muslim-Arab, Spanish, Portuguese, French and British empires made the world we live in. Others, like the Persian, Mongol and German ruled large swathes for long periods, but left little, if anything, behind. It has been said that the British acquired their empire in a fit of absent-mindedness; much the same could be said of America's recent hegemony.

American imperialism can be divided into three periods. First came territorial expansionism to make way for resettlement. Once independent of Britain, the colonies launched unsuccessful wars against Canada, spread across the continent into settled Mexican territory and engaged in genocidal wars against the American Indians.

The second stage was the war against Spain, which gave the US traditional style colonies: Puerto Rico, the Philippines (where 200,000 citizens were killed in wars of resistance) and large numbers of Pacific Islands to add to Hawaii and create a Pacific shield. The third stage is American hegemony, spreading into Europe, the Near and Middle East, parts of Asia and Latin America... The experience of the Cuban missile crisis, communist rule in Nicaragua and communist terror in El Salvador in a shrinking world make it harder for the US to relinquish its levels of involvement. A test will come when Castro leaves the controls.

NATO, originally devised a defensive weapon against the very real threat of Stalinist expansion, has turned into a major instrument of American domination. This need not necessarily have been so, and was undertaken without a national debate in the US or Europe. Whereas the previous functions of NATO were clearly spelled out, its present objectives are clouded in euphemisms. The first question any military alliance should answer - who is the enemy? - is left unanswered. The first victims were the Serbs, subjected to a crippling blockade and then bombardment; the second have been the Macedonians, whose statehood and identity are now in question. The first beneficiaries have been the ultra-nationalist and indeed clero-fascist Croats and the Slav and

Albanian Muslims. NATO has transformed Kosovo-Metohija into an Albanian-ruled criminal fiefdom.

The US decision to convert NATO from a defensive alliance into an instrument of hegemony, and its consequent pogrom against the Serbs and generous support for Slav and Albanian Muslim expansion, represented a turning point - which requires explanation.

To some extent, the temptation to use diplomatic and military power to gain an expanded share of Caspian oil following relaxation of Moscow's control over states in the basin - Azerbajdjan, Kazakhstan, Turkmenistan, Georgia and Armenia - played a part. But one cannot rule out the role of bribery. The USA is a corrupt country, not more so than many others but not less so either. It is commonplace for the criminal underworld even more than legitimate big business to control politicians, judges, police and government at state and city levels. In the past, this has been done mainly to protect them in their criminal or business activities, although the Mafia's provision of sexual partners to Jack Kennedy and his brothers must have had political overtones which America is coy to trace.

However, the Croats and Albanians are another matter. The wartime Croat Ustasi government imposed by the Germans not only killed off hundreds of thousands of Serbs and all the Jews it could lay its hands on, but confiscated all Jewish property. This wealth was smuggled out of the country after Germany's defeat with the aid of the Vatican and Swiss banks, first to Argentina and then to Canada and the United States. The money was used among other things for political activities leading to the eventual establishment of a semi-fascist xenophobic state in Croatia with German aid, from which any remaining Serbs were expelled with NATO help. It was Croat Ustasi money which fed into illegal party accounts held by Kohl and his colleagues and subsequently bought their pardons. In the USA, this money went as 'campaign contributions' - Americanese for bribes - and helped the Croatian campaign for the break-up of Yugoslavia and the creation of a Greater Croatia from which rooted Serb communities were expelled *en masse*, several thousand being killed in the process.

The Albanians went even further. In recent decades, they have become one of the largest criminal communities in the world, matching the Sicilians. Their part in the heroin traffic from Afghanistan across to Italy and the USA is no longer second to that of the Turkish gangs. They control prostitution all over Europe. In the United States the Albanian-owned businesses serve as important links in drug trafficking and money-laundering. They finance the lavishly funded American-Albanian Political Action Committee. Politicians who have benefited from Albanian Mafia largesse over the years included Dole, Lieberman, Hillary Clinton (who bullied her husband into bombing Serbia), McCain, and the late Tom Lantos, among others.

On America's past form we can expect the U.S. and its allies-cum-clients to continue their de facto war against Serbia in Raska ("Sanjak") and Vojvodina. In a curious way the nineteenth century is being replayed out before our eyes. The great powers are intervening at will and with impunity but justifying themselves in the name of the "international community." (The latter has become the modern equivalent of Rousseau's "general will," which means the will of the person talking.) The Congress of Berlin has even been mentioned, approvingly, without the consideration that it was a step on the way towards the catastrophe of 1914.

The U.S-led NATO intervention in the Balkans had not been designed to defend or further the West's vital interests. It has visibly done the opposite. Western intervention in Yugoslavia has come as a result of *Western crisis:* first, the vacuum caused by de-Christianization, and secondly *hubris* brought on by Soviet imperialism's collapse. "The American Century" and "The New World Order" contain a new cultural paradigm: materialistic, anti-traditional, and hegemonistic.

This megalomania is a form of madness, nothing new in world history. This the Serbs know to their cost, as they still suffer from the consequences of the Fourth Crusade and Louis XIV's intervention to prevent the Habsburgs' liberation of the eastern Balkans in the early eighteenth century, as well as the Western powers' Turkophile policies in the nineteenth.

The Yugoslav imbroglio is a symptom of these deeper ills in the Western world. Western public opinion is beginning to sense this, if not actually recognize and understand it. To help them to do this, Serbs must put their own intellectual and spiritual house in order.

The pursuit of World Importance for the sake of World Importance is the Great Temptation in human history, the path of ruin that winds from Xerxes, the Persian King of Kings, to Hitler, the Austrian corporal-tyrant. It is the path which George Washington forbade America ever to take. The American People will never choose it, but can they prevent it? The American foreign policy elite is locking itself onto this path, and their co-conspirators in the media corporations are calling it a pilgrimage. Bosnia was the acid test. They knew why they should not go in; they knew the damage it would do to their oldest alliances; but they could not resist. The combination of high moral purpose, however fudged up by the media, and the chance to show Europe that Only America Decides was just too intoxicating.

The United States is still powerful, but a law of history is that power tends to generate countervailing power. We can do little more than guard against arrogance and over-extension and minimize the pointless sacrifices they usually entail. I am proud to have taken part in this struggle, the struggle to bring the powerful to their senses before they plunge into reckless, ruthless folly. This struggle carries no guarantee of success, for it is the quest for sanity that epitomizes the struggle of suffering humanity throughout the ages.

# Washington's Destabilizing Crusade

**Doug Bandow**[1]

A decade ago the United States intervened in the Balkans, a region of no strategic interest to America. The alliance triumphed, naturally, but the peace has proved to be harder than the war. Europe is still living with the consequences of that ill-considered aggression. In February 2008 Kosovo declared its independence, with Washington's support. The number of recognitions has stalled, however, despite U.S. pressure on friends and allies around the globe, and Russia used the Kosovo precedent to justify its war with Georgia in support of South Ossetia. Serbia obtained a United Nations General Assembly vote to take its case to the World Court. The conflict remains frozen, only with new flashpoints, most notably the status of the Serbian community in Kosovo's north.

U.S. policy desperately needs reconsideration. Despite a foreign policy at times ostentatiously at odds with that of his predecessor, President George W. Bush closely followed the Clinton administration's Balkans policies and illusions. Now the responsibility lies with President Barack Obama. He won the presidential election running against Bush administration policy, yet so far his international approach has emphasized continuity with the previous administration. And with Hillary Clinton at the State Department, little change is likely in U.S. attempts to micromanage Balkan affairs.

Throughout much of the Cold War, the U.S. implicitly backed Yugoslavia against the Soviet Union. When the former began to split apart in the early 1990s,

---

1 Doug Bandow is a Senior Fellow at the Cato Institute. A former Special Assistant to President Ronald Reagan, he is the author of several books, including *Foreign Follies: America's New Global Empire* (Xulon).

Washington, in contrast to Europe, sought to slow the dissolution process. But President Bill Clinton eventually saw the Balkans as the perfect laboratory for turning U.S. foreign policy into a form of "international social work," and took American policy in a very different direction.

President Clinton shifted American foreign policy by disconnecting interest from policy, intervening where the U.S. had no geopolitical interests at stake. For instance, the administration pushed to expand the United Nations mission in Somalia from food relief to nation-building. Washington ousted the military rulers of Haiti.

But Somalia soured official Washington on attempting to save Africa. When Sierra Leone imploded, resulting in a quarter million deaths, Washington did nothing more than issue statements. Washington policy-makers seemed unsurprised by such violence in such places, and were not inclined to intervene. Some unkind observers suggested that latent racism was responsible for the difference in approach.

Clinton administration policymakers viewed Europe very differently, however. With no major power willing to go to war over Yugoslavia's break-up – in sharp contrast to the events preceding World War I, in which alliances proved to be transmission belts of war – the U.S. could have safely ignored the conflict in the Balkans. But President Clinton saw an opportunity to burnish the administration's humanitarian credentials.

Moreover, Yugoslavia provided a convenient enemy, unlike Sierra Leone. Secretary of State Madeleine Albright admitted that her framework was Munich. The facts that six decades had passed and the circumstances could not have been more different – Slobodan Milosevic, though a nasty piece of work, was no Adolf Hitler, and tiny bedraggled Serbia was not remotely comparable to Nazi Germany – apparently escaped her. She believed that only American entry in the war could prevent Europe from suffering a historical relapse with who knows what imagined consequences.

Thus, on humanitarian grounds Washington supported every group which sought to secede from the central Yugoslavian state. The principle of ethnic self-determination, harkening back to Woodrow Wilson's famed Fourteen Points, became central to U.S. foreign policy.

However, self-determination stopped whenever Serbs sought to apply the principle. Slovenes, Croats, Bosnian Muslims, and Macedonians (and later Montenegrins) were entitled to secede from Serb-dominated Yugoslavia. But Serbs were never entitled to secede from other political units, most notably Croatia and Bosnia. The Clinton administration implicitly believed in collective punishment: the perceived aggressors would not be allowed to take advantage of the humanitarian principles available to others. Never mind that Croats and Muslims perpetrated their own share of atrocities, sometimes against each other. Most notably, the Clinton administration did not protest Croatian ethnic cleansing of Serbs from their historic homeland in that seceding nation, refusing even to term Zagreb's brutal military offensive ethnic cleansing. Federalism and stable borders became defining issues whenever Serbs constituted the minority population.

American policy towards Kosovo reflected the same attitude: outside intervention was necessary to stop a new Hitler and self-determination applied to anyone in revolt against Serbs but not to Serbs. As before, reality on the ground was irrelevant. Washington would engage in social engineering to make the Balkans, if not the world, a better place.

Milosevic was a thug and Serbian forces behaved badly throughout Yugoslavia's break-up, but the fighting in Kosovo was no worse than in any other guerrilla conflict. Consider how Turkey, a full NATO ally and EU aspirant, treated its Kurdish minority—nearly 40,000 dead and hundreds of thousands displaced in a brutal guerrilla war. The Kosovo Liberation Army responded to official brutality, but committed its own atrocities in return, targeting Serb security forces and Albanian "collaborators." U.S. diplomats even referred to the KLA as "terrorist."

The Clinton administration made a symbolic attempt to restore peace, summoning the contending sides to Rambouillet, France. Under the guise of "negotiating" Washington attempted to impose a settlement that would have given the ethnic Albanians everything except immediate independence.[2] Serbia would have had to accept the status of a conquered province, agreeing to free transit by NATO forces through the entire country. It was an accord that no sovereign state could sign, as the Clinton administration well knew.

Since Belgrade refused to accept rule from Washington or Brussels, the U.S. led the world's greatest military alliance made up of most of the globe's industrialized powers against the small, isolated Balkan power that had been wracked by years of secessionist conflict and ravaged by Western sanctions. The outcome was never in doubt, though the lack of allied planning was stunning. The Clinton administration had assumed that a few days of bombing would cause Yugoslavia's acquiescence, but had no Plan B when Milosevic refused to yield. After 78 days of bombing Belgrade finally gave up Kosovo but refused to otherwise compromise its security.

---

2  See article by Dr. Ronald Hatchett.

Of course, once NATO defenestrated Serbian security forces from Kosovo, the final disposition of the territory was obvious. Although UN Resolution 1244 assumed continued Serbian sovereignty over Kosovo, providing for "a political process designed to determine Kosovo's future status," the allies never intended serious negotiations without preconditions. Rather, Washington clearly communicated to ethnic Albanians that independence would be the final result. Negotiations were simply for show to disguise Serbia's expected surrender. Thus, the ethnic Albanians had no reason to consider settling for anything short of independence.

They did offer to respect the rights of ethnic Serbs – respect, however, not demonstrated when ethnic Albanians kicked out a quarter of a million Serbs and other minorities, including Roma and Jews, after the war, and destroyed Serb homes, churches, and monasteries in another round of violence in March 2004. But the Albanians offered nothing else, demanding nothing less than independence for all of Kosovo, even in the northern areas heavily populated by Serbs.

The newly elected democratic government in Belgrade responded by offering a number of approaches with largely unrestricted autonomy. Nevertheless, the U.S. and leading European states declared Serbia to be the intransigent party, "obstructing" and "stonewalling" a settlement. In short, the "negotiations" were a sham designed to justify a decision made long before to grant Kosovo independence.

Obviously, there was no perfect solution, one which would fully satisfy both sides. The Milosevic government had behaved brutally and after the ouster of Serb forces the ethnic Albanians saw no reason to again recognize Belgrade's sovereignty. But minority Serbs had no more reason to believe Pristina's promises of protection and inclusion.

Nor could the Serbs take the West's promise to maintain outside oversight seriously. After all, both spasms of ethnic Albanian violence occurred *during allied occupation*. In mid-1999, even as tens of thousands of people were fleeing Kosovo, Secretary Albright was telling the Council of Foreign Relations that the allied occupation force "takes seriously its mandate to protect Kosovars, including Serbs. And its effectiveness will increase as deployment continues, and demilitarization gains steam." It would have been a bad joke were people not at that very moment being driven from their homes.

The territory seemed no closer to ethnic reconciliation in 2004, when thousands more ethnic Serbs were killed, injured, and displaced. Derek Chappell, spokesman for the UN military force, UNMIK, observed: "some in the Kosovo Albanian leadership believe that by cleansing all remaining Serbs from the area ... and destroying Serbian cultural sites, they can present the international community with a fait accompli." Even the International Crisis Group (ICG), which believes in a multilateral response to every problem, acknowledged that the rampage "shattered international confidence that the Albanians were committed to a tolerant society" – confidence that obviously was never justified.

No one was punished for their crimes, and the Organization for Security and Cooperation in Europe (OSCE) acknowledged that "This relatively weak response ... not only contributes to the impression of impunity among the population for such kinds of ethnically motivated crimes but may also be considered inadequate to prevent similar acts of public disorder in the future."

While the Pristina government did not publicly support the attacks, the ethnic Albanian political leadership, made up of former guerrilla leaders, some accused of wartime atrocities, likely had the same goals as in 1999. Acknowledged the ICG: "With no vision for the future of Serbs in Kosovo, one might suspect that the latent Albanian hope is that they will all eventually sell out and leave." The *Washington Post* captured this attitude when it quoted an 18-year-old ethnic Albanian cigarette vendor: "Really, the Serbs ought to go back to Serbia."

The ethnic Albanian leadership also has been implicated in the explosion of organized crime, including drug dealing, money laundering, and sex trafficking. Maria Kalavis, UNICEF's regional director for Southeast Europe, recently warned, "We know that child trafficking within Kosovo's borders is on the rise." Some have referred to Kosovo as the "black hole" of Europe.

Although Islam was never much of a factor in the past, radical Islam appears to be on the rise. There has been an influx of Saudi money, which has underwritten many of the 200 mosques constructed since 1999; on a recent trip I saw a Saudi flag flying over a mosque. Christian converts have been threatened and some analysts believe that terrorists have infiltrated the Balkans through Kosovo as well as Bosnia. Thomas Gambill, a onetime OSCE security official, observed: "My biggest concern has always been the incursion of radical Islam into the area." "Sex, crime, terrorism, it's all there," one U.S. diplomat told me.

All told, Kosovo's record was at best disappointing after a decade of supposed tutelage in democracy by the "international community." At a 2006 congressional hearing, Charles English of the State Department stated: "Discrimination remains a serious problem. Access to public services is uneven. Incidents of harassment still occur. Freedom of movement is limited. And too many minorities still feel unsafe in Kosovo."

Even Javier Solana, the European Union's foreign policy head, and Kai Eide, the UN's special envoy, criticized Kosovo's failure to meet specified political benchmarks. In 2006 the ICG, which continued to push for an independent Kosovo, warned that "The international community's immediate priority is to avert a new exodus of Serbs, new Albanian-Serb clashes, or a new wave of burning houses and churches."

In November 2007 the European Commission released a report that concluded that "some progress was made in consolidating government" but "working tools for an efficient government" still had "to be enhanced and fully applied" – more than eight years after the territory's *de facto* separation from Serbia. Unsurprising, given the level of criminal activity by former guerrillas, the Commission warned that "corruption is still widespread and remains a major problem." Moreover, "Civil servants are still vulnerable to political interference, corrupt practices and nepotism." As for the judiciary, "The backlog of cases is increasing, with more than 50,000 civil cases and over 36,000 criminal cases pending." There also is a backlog in war crime cases, which are "hampered by the unwillingness of the local population to testify."

Overall, explained the Commission, "little progress has been made in the promotion and enforcement of human rights. The administration is not able to ensure the full implementation of human rights standards." The commitment of the Pristina authorities to resolving more than 2000 missing persons cases "is not sufficient to achieve objective and efficient investigations," complained the Commission. Further, "no investigations or court proceedings on torture or ill-treatment [of prisoners] have yet taken place." Minorities and other vulnerable groups "face restrictions in exercising their right to freedom of assembly and association across Kosovo." In fact, the police or armed forces must always guard minority gatherings. Finally, "only limited progress" was achieved in promoting religious liberty. Indeed, the Commission concluded, "Religious freedom is not fully respected."

Kosovo hardly sounded ready for prime-time.

Compromises were possible—overlapping EU, Kosovo, and Serbian citizenship and partition north of the Ibar River were two leading candidates—which might have won grudging agreement on both sides. No one would have been happy with the result, but both sides could have "moved on," in common parlance. But rather than encourage genuine negotiations, the U.S. preferred to employ the principle "the Serbs always lose."

What was supposed to be a pleasant bit of Kabuki theater, with everyone playing their assigned role to reach the predetermined outcome, quickly fell apart. Both the Serbs and Russians balked. Russian opposition apparently surprised the U.S. When another year of meaningless "negotiation" ended, Washington and like-minded European states decided to make another end-run around the United Nations and back Kosovo's unilateral independence.

The success of Washington's gambit remains in doubt. The current number of recognitions is under 60, only a few more than the number of countries which recognize the Western Sahara (claimed by Morocco). Even many Islamic countries which worry about challenges to their own territorial integrity have refused to sign on: Washington's claim that Kosovo's status is "unique" and not a precedent is too self-serving for anyone to take seriously. Serbia vows continued resistance and Russia insists that Kosovo will never join the UN. If the ICJ rules for Belgrade some nations might even reverse their recognitions of Pristina.

But Washington policymakers have had no apparent second thoughts. Their justifications sound the same as before, though reinforced with a heavy dose of self-righteousness. In her official statement on Kosovo's independence in 2008, former Secretary of State Condoleezza Rice harkened back to NATO's intervention "to end brutal attacks on the Kosovar Albanian population." Since then, she said, Kosovo "has built its own democratic institutions" and Washington welcomed its commitments "to embrace multi-ethnicity as a fundamental principle of good governance, and to welcome a period of international supervision." President George W. Bush said much the same, stating: "Kosovo committed itself to the highest standards of democracy, including freedom and tolerance and justice for citizens of all ethnic backgrounds."

It is hard to take such arguments seriously. The guerrilla conflict was brutal, but no more so than America's Civil War, after which the seceding territory was forcibly retained. Far more Kurds have died at Turkish hands in long-running hostilities, but the Kurds remain part of Turkey. The U.S. has never held that the relative bitterness of a conflict a decade before determined a territory's juridical status. Moreover, Secretary Rice appeared to be the only person who believed in the effectiveness of Kosovo's so-called democratic institutions.

If Secretary Rice's arguments were considered dispositive, then they applied with even greater force to the ethnic Serbs in Kosovo. The Serbs (as well as Roma and other minorities) can point to recent brutality and oppression as warranting independence. And by remaining in Serbia they would remain in a democracy which used the ballot box to overthrow Milosevic. What more is needed, under Washington's rationale?

Even more bizarre was Secretary Rice's claim that Kosovo maintains a multi-ethnic state. Today the territory is multi-ethnic only in the sense that the majority ethnic

Albanians were unable to kick out all of the ethnic Serbs and the Western states want to force the remaining ethnic Serbs to stay. A truly multi-ethnic society does not exist.

Moreover, the consecutive secessions from united Yugoslavia, all supported by the U.S. and many European states, ran against Washington's supposed principle of maintaining multi-ethnic nations. It is more than bizarre to cite multi-ethnicity as a rationale for denying the final oppressed minority the right to secede—which, in this case, simply means remaining within the mother country. The ill precedent of dividing countries along ethnic lines was set long ago and has been reinforced by Kosovo's claimed independence by the ethnic Albanian majority.

Another argument, advanced by Undersecretary of State Nicholas Burns in 2008, was that there is positive good in creating another majority Muslim state in Europe. He explained: "Kosovo is going to be a vastly majority Muslim state .... And we think it is a very positive step that this Muslim state, Muslim majority state, has been created today."

Muslims have the same right of self-determination as does everyone else, of course, but why should be establishing a Muslim government America's or Europe's goal? Europe is finding the task of thwarting terrorism and blending cultures to be more difficult than Washington acknowledges. Although the credible claims of jihadist and terrorist activity centered in Bosnia and Kosovo are of most concern to Europe, the U.S. also should worry. Recognizing Kosovo is not likely to dampen potential conflict.

Then there is the issue of stability. In 2008 President George W. Bush asserted that "our position is that its status must be resolved in order for the Balkans to be stable." His successors advance identical or similar claims.

While an independence deal accepted by Kosovo *and* Serbia, as well as the U.S., Europe, *and* Russia would encourage stability, Kosovo's unilateral declaration has destabilized the region. Serbia has drifted towards Russia as even centrist politicians in Serbia affirmed their opposition to Western policy. Serbia's politics has grown more fractious. Any attempt to coerce Serbs within Kosovo to submit to Pristina is likely to generate violent resistance. The divide between Russia and the U.S. and EU has grown.

Indeed, Moscow put the West's principles to work in the Caucasus. Russia may have been cynical in supporting Abkhazia's and South Ossetia's self-determination, but the latter two have as much if not more justification in declaring independence as did Kosovo. Washington's complaints about Russia violating Georgia's territorial integrity during the brief war in August 2008 could generate only a horse laugh in Belgrade and

Moscow. The U.S. set the rules in Kosovo: Washington could act as judge and jury in adjudicating independence claims in other countries and violently dismember another sovereign state if it chose to do so. Russia has simply adopted these rules as its own.

Secretary Rice undoubtedly believed that "It's time to move forward." What could be more convenient for Washington's policy ends? But Kosovo never was part of America. Tell the Spanish to yield their Basque territory or Catalonia. Tell Hungary to forget about land parceled out to the victors by the Versailles Treaty. Tell Kurds to accept rule from Ankara. Tell Serbs in Bosnia and Albanians in Macedonia to abandon their dreams of independence. And tell people in scores of nations around the world to forget their desire for self-determination.

Kosovo's impact is likely to ultimately reach far beyond the Balkans. Taiwan cheerfully recognized Kosovo, to China's chagrin. Costa Rica recognized both Kosovo and Palestine. Similar cases are likely to multiply. Hypocritical claims by U.S. (and EU) officials that Kosovo is unique fall on deaf ears of peoples wishing to be free and independent.

Indeed, rather than discouraging other claims of independence, the American insistence that Kosovo is unique is likely to spur groups desiring recognition to replicate the Kosovo formula: violently resist, target collaborators, encourage a government crackdown, and demand foreign intervention. The U.S. and EU have written an official playbook for separatism.

The West's hypocrisy regarding the self-determination for Kosovo's remaining Serbs through partition of Kosovo is even more grotesque. Undersecretary Burns declared simply "We will not support any form of partition." He added that "the great majority of countries would not stand for that," even though the great majority of countries have refused to recognize Kosovo. As justification he harkened back to the brutalities of the 1998-1999 conflict. Set aside the fact that the KLA was not a group of innocents. Serb misbehavior might explain why Kosovo should be independent; it cannot explain why majority Serb areas should be forced to remain in Kosovo, especially since ethnic Albanians already have repaid past brutality in kind.

The refusal to consider any compromise suggests that Washington – at least the part of the bureaucracy today concerned about Kosovo – remains ruled by Madeleine Albright's Munich mindset. Leading Serbs privately acknowledge that partition is the most obvious strategy to bridge the ethnic divide. Washington's refusal to consider the slightest compromise indicates that the support for Kosovo's independence is ideological.

U.S. policy retains an otherworldly quality. American officials seem genuinely bewildered why Serbs are so angry. While she was explaining how the U.S. was working to strip Serbia of 15 percent of its territory, Secretary Rice asserted: "The United States takes this opportunity to reaffirm our friendship with Serbia." Without irony, President Bush claimed: "the Serbian people can know that they have a friend in America." That dismembering their nation would be viewed as an unfriendly act by Serbs apparently never occurred to Secretary Rice or President Bush. They appeared to the world to be naïve fools, far worse than being seen as callous cynics.

Now it is up to the Obama administration.

For more than a decade Washington has led the bungling in the Balkans. The U.S. torpedoed one of the early attempts to settle the Bosnian crisis, the Lisbon Plan. Years of war and tens of thousands of dead resulted: much of that blood was on the hands of Washington policymakers. But the U.S. government continues to put ideology before reality.

Returning to the status quo might not be a viable option, but neither is pretending that recognizing Kosovo independence will yield regional stability. The U.S. and EU could still convene a conference, harkening back to the Congress of Berlin and similar gatherings, to conduct genuine negotiations with the goal of achieving an acceptable compromise. Otherwise, Kosovo's declaration of independence is likely to prove to be just another milestone in continuing regional strife.

# "Independent" Kosovo's Failure and the Mystery of the U.S. Balkan Policy

*James George Jatras*[1]

The fact that after a whole year the supposedly "independent state" of Kosovo has been recognized by only 55 of the United Nations' 192 member states -- many of them small and insignificant -- is a great failure for Washington's policy. It was asserted by independence proponents in Washington that immediately over 100 countries would grant recognition, and that the Kosovo and Metohija problem would be "solved". Most members of the EU in particular were pressured or tricked into following along, and many of them clearly regret their mistake.

Meanwhile the roster of important countries that have rejected the illegal unilateral declaration of independence by the gaggle of terrorists and Mafiosi ensconced in Pristina remains in place a year later: Russia, China, India, Indonesia, Brazil, South Africa, Mexico, Argentina, most of Latin America, most of Africa, even most of the Islamic world. Kosovo will never be a member of the United Nations. As even its most ardent promoters concede, Kosovo one year after is anything but a functional state. The independence project has failed, however much its architects try to fool themselves to the contrary.

IT IS BY NO MEANS "OVER" – The battle for Kosovo goes on and must be continued by the most vigorous means. Strong diplomatic, military, and economic measures are needed to further pressure the illegal and nonviable entity. These include

---

1 James Jatras is Director of the American Council for Kosovo in Washington, D.C. (www.savekosovo.org)

downgrading diplomatic ties with recognizing countries, military exercises in southern Serbia, and selective interruptions in crossing between Kosovo and the rest of Serbia. Some of these I have recommended before, and in my opinion they can and should be taken at this late date.

But even in the absence of such measures Serbia is, all in all, winning. There has been some disagreement of supporters of the Serbian position as to whether Belgrade should have forced a vote in the General Assembly on referring the Kosovo question to the International Court of Justice. On balance, I think it was a good move. The spectacle of Washington's losing the votes of almost all he countries that have granted recognition and securing support only from a mighty coalition of Albania, Marshall Islands, Nauru, Palau, and Micronesia – an unprecedented and humiliating isolation – was alone worth the price of admission.

The ICJ cannot fail to rule in Serbia's favor unless it is completely corrupted and prepared to unravel the entire international system. Generally, the Court has not acted in that manner. To be sure, the opinion will be only advisory, and no country will be bound by the outcome – a factor that applies to Serbia in event the decision is unfavorable. (Even if that happens, the Court would be certain to be divided along political, not judicial lines, degrading whatever authority an ICJ opinion might otherwise have.) In any case, while the decision is pending, recognitions will continue at a snail's pace if at all. If the decision is favorable for Serbia, some counties will find it a convenient excuse to withdraw their recognitions.

The current Belgrade government's agreement on the "six points" for letting EULEX into northern Kosovo was a mistake. However, the Albanians and their supporters are not happy either. The result has been perpetuation of the uncertainty over who really is in charge; in any case, it is not the Albanians.

Let's look further at the plus side: In the Security Council, Moscow and Beijing have refused to allow the UN to slink out of Kosovo and turn its functions over to EULEX. The province's Serbian enclaves remain outside control of the criminal and terrorist Kosovo Liberation Army administration. Overstretched in Iraq and Afghanistan, Washington cannot, by itself, take action to impose the Albanians' "authority" over Kosovo's Serbs by force. While a provocation to justify an "Operation Storm"-like assault cannot be ruled out, Washington's European allies hardly are likely to help the U.S. start a new Balkan war to do so. In short, the accelerating slide of American hegemony worldwide has narrowed Washington's Kosovo options even further, and that slide will track with that of the American economy.

But while the Kosovo project is being revealed as the fraud it always was, the fact is that the death blow has yet to be delivered. It should have been months ago, and it is shameful that it was not. Having failed to finish the "Kosova" monster in its cradle, Serbia remains vulnerable to a sudden shift in the wrong direction. This danger is especially acute with the accession of the Barack Obama Administration and the return, like a blast of stale air, of names from the 1990s: Hillary Clinton, Joseph Biden, Richard Holbrooke. Lately the usual suspects – Holbrooke and Paddy Ashdown, Morton Abramowitz and Daniel Serwer – have taken to the op-ed pages to insist on America to re-focus on the Balkans (translation: beat up on Serbia some more).

In short, a decade after the NATO aggression, and Washington's championing perhaps the most blatant violation of the norms of international behavior since the 1938 carve-up of Czechoslovakia (perhaps worse, since in end Prague capitulated but Belgrade has refused) – the battle for Kosovo goes on.

EXPLAINING THE INEXPLICABLE – Nonetheless, even after the passage of ten years, the question lingers: *Why?* Why did the most supposedly enlightened democratic countries in the world do this? Even more so, why did the self-anointed "Leader of the Free World" insist on it? Indeed, having been for many years a policy analyst at the U.S. Senate and an observer of regional phenomena since before the outbreak of the new Balkan Wars in 1991, I have to confess that I am *still* unable to explain satisfactorily the motives behind American behavior.

A large part of that inability derives from the fact that the behavior of the U.S. has been so completely irrational that it defies coherent explanation. Also, the unfolding of American policy has been so influenced by incidental and external factors that the course, if not the motivations, of U.S. policy might have been different if those factors had been different. These include the internal conflict among the Europeans faced with Germany's 1991 demand for recognition of Slovene and Croatian secessions from Yugoslavia, that in 1999 Milosevic settled the Kosovo war how and when he did, and that Moscow was so supine in the 1990s and today is anything but.

All that having been said, it is nonetheless possible to lay out certain elements that have influenced American policy and have, in the aggregate, helped produce what we see today:

First, **The power of money and lobbying in Washington**: The influence of organized political lobbies in Washington never should be underestimated. Anti-Serb lobbies, notably Albanian-Americans, have been well-funded and well-placed, literally, for decades. Meanwhile, today as in the past, the "Serbian lobby" hardly exists. This has contributed mightily to the black and white morality play – to which Americans are notoriously amenable – in which the Serbs were and still are evil incarnate, and their opponents blameless victims. Well before the outbreak of hostilities in 1991, the Serbs had already been branded the bad guys, prior to any accusations of so-called "Serb atrocities" that constituted an *ex post facto* justification for our anti-Serb policies. As a product of money and lobbying, combined with media reinforcement, much false information is accepted as unquestionable fact, which colors our approach to all future developments.

This fact also needs to be seen in a larger regional context: Lobbies in Washington by ethnic groups in the United States, mainly those representing communities of Central European interests who lost out in World War II – Croatians, Albanians, Hungarians, Latvians, Estonians, west Ukrainian Uniates, and so forth – were highly influential throughout the Cold War, mainly in the Republican Party. This "World War II Losers Club" was able to present itself to Americans as simply anti-communist while in fact promoting their own ethnic agendas. Perhaps it would not be reading too much into it to see an element of Polish anti-Russian sentiment in Zbigniew Brżezinski's call that Russia be broken up into three parts.

In the Balkans, Washington has adopted every Axis ally from World War II, and the map of the region is coming to resemble that of 1943. In recent years this assembly has been augmented by new, specifically anti-Russian influences, such as lobbies for Chechen separatists, as well as paid American agents of "Orange" Ukraine and "Rose" Georgia. These lobbies have in turn received powerful support from political groups, notably the so-called "neoconservatives," which I will describe further below. The result has been a black and white morality play – to which Americans are notoriously amenable – in which Russians and communities perceived to be related to them, primarily by religion, especially Serbs, are perceived as adversaries and responsible for all regional conflicts. As a product of money and lobbying, combined with media reinforcement, much false information is accepted as unquestionable fact, which colors our approach to all future developments. In short, we have not only an identifiable Russophobia, but related Serbophobia, even an occasional whiff of Hellenophobia, and collectively what amounts to Pravoslavophobia.

Second, **Inertia:** In politics no one ever admits he is wrong about anything. Like the NKVD, the U.S. government never makes mistakes. Having committed to a certain version of events, and a consequent justification of U.S. policies, it is unthinkable that any responsible political actor will go back to suggest we might have misunderstood, or even falsified, the facts, or that our actions were misguided. More damaging, having set our regional course on the basis of falsehoods, future decisions are bound to be consistent with it.

This tendency is reinforced by the fact that the foreign policy community in Washington is small and closely integrated, almost entirely sharing the same worldview, and hardly changes from administration to administration, regardless of which party is in power. That is why, for example, one hears so much talk with respect to Kosovo that it is "the last piece of unfinished business in the Balkans" – which means, of course, that its solution must reflect the anti-Serb formula applied in the past, because to do otherwise would call into doubt our previous actions. This tendency is further reinforced by the fact that many of the principals in the Bush Administration's Balkan policies are Clinton holdovers, who of course have a personal stake in defending their past actions. Under the Obama Administration, the whole cabal is back with a vengeance.

Third, **Islamophilia**: Deriving in part from American support for Islamic forces going back at least to the Afghan war against the Soviet Union, and contrary to conventional accusations that the U.S. is hostile to Islam, our favoritism towards Islamic forces has been clear and consistent. This even meant, for example, Washington's benign pre-2001 attitude toward the Taliban, going back even before their advent to power in 1996 with the support of the U.S.-allied Pakistani Inter-Services Intelligence and Saudi funding. In expectation of a Turkmenistan-Afghanistan-Pakistan pipeline (an eastern counterpart to Baku-Çeyhan), the sole U.S. concern was whether we could "do business" with the Taliban – and more importantly, keep Caspian energy out of Russian hands.

The attacks that took place in New York and Washington in 2001, far from reversing such pattern of pro-Islamic favoritism, helped turn that pattern into an obsession. Continuing up to the present, the pronouncements from American officials regarding Islam as a religion of "peace and tolerance" – in which the factor of jihad ideology is ignored in favor of reference to a generic "terrorism" committed by "evildoers" – display the extent to which U.S. policymakers became fixated on the notion that victory in the misnamed "war on terror" could only be achieved by getting the Muslim world on our side. This is in sharp contrast to the blunt and factual warnings of Prime Minister Vladimir Putin regarding the danger of the campaign to revive the global *Khilafah* (the caliphate). It also has been reflected in U.S. overt and covert support for Chechen terrorists, such as the 2004 grant of asylum to the so-called Chechen "foreign minister" Ilyas Akhmadov, even against the protests of the U.S. Department of Homeland Security. One can imagine the reaction in Washington if Russia gave asylum to a jihad commander from Iraq. More to the point, it is hard to imagine Russia doing such a thing.

Fourth, **Global hegemony**: A central element of Washington's policy must be attributed to the post-Cold War notion of the United States as the sole surviving superpower, cast in the role of what some influential advocates have called "benevolent global hegemony."

This concept has particular application to Europe, where it is an article of faith in Washington that no security decision can be taken without U.S. approval, and preferably, sponsorship. NATO, an entirely American-controlled body, must dominate European security. To give some examples: This is why Washington broke its pledge that NATO would not be extended further east at the time of the 1990 reuniting of Germany and the voluntary Soviet withdrawal of its forces from the Warsaw Pact countries that followed soon after. This is an important reason why Washington encouraged its Bosnian Muslim clients to reject the European-sponsored Vance-Owen and Owen-Stoltenberg peace plans but insisted on acceptance of the barely different Dayton agreement, which bore a "Made in USA" stamp. This likewise explains Washington's determination that Moscow cannot be allowed to "win" on Kosovo, notwithstanding the obvious fact that the U.S. position is inconsistent with any commonly understood standard of international legality and that the Russians are upholding those very standards. It also applies to Washington's demand that Poland and the Czech Republic accept a supposedly defensive missile system to protect European countries from nonexistent Iranian weapons, even though no one in these countries is asking for such protection.

It is also evidenced in Washington's support for the Saakashvili regime's inhuman aggression against South Ossetia and Abkhazia, which risked direct confrontation between American and Russian soldiers, something that both the U.S. and Soviet Union carefully avoided during the Cold War. Most dangerously, it is why Washington is adamant that Georgia and Ukraine must be members of NATO even though most European members of NATO are not very eager for that outcome and in Ukraine all polls show most people are opposed. So much for democracy.

The confluence of these ingredients – lobbying, inertia, Islamophilia, hegemony – provides if not a complete explanation, perhaps at least frames a context in which to discuss the motivation and effects of American Balkan policy for over a decade. Add to these one other element that is unique to the recently departed Administration which made the final push for Kosovo's independence: the brittleness of President Bush's personality, which treated every negative policy development as a test of his character, integrity, and perseverance. One could cite any number of examples, both foreign and domestic, to illustrate this quality, from support for his amnesty bill to the Dubai ports fiasco to his unwillingness to abandon politically nonviable appointees.

FUTILE APPEASEMENT – Having decided that America's role as midwife for "moderate," "democratic" Islam is not only possible but necessary, there was never much prospect he would ever reexamine his assumptions. With respect to our topic he now has made a point of digging in his heels by announcing in Tirana in June 2007: "At some point in time, sooner rather than later, you got to say 'enough's enough, Kosovo's independent.'" And then... well, then the Albanians stole his watch right off his wrist.

Because these the second two factors identified above – Washington's pro-Islamic imperative and the lust for global domination that has defined U.S. policy since the end of the Cold War – are the most potent of the four, further elaboration is in order.

Washington's supine posture in the face of the global jihad has been as overt as it is craven. For example, in June 2007 President Bush visited Washington's Islamic Center, during which, standing in his stocking feet, he repeated his call for a Palestinian state, touted U.S. support for Muslims in Bosnia and Kosovo, characterized jihadists as betrayers of the Islamic faith (as if the opinion of a *kafir* counts for anything), stated his intention to appoint a "special envoy" to the Organization of the Islamic Conference, and expressed Americans' collective "appreciation for a faith that has enriched civilization for centuries." (In the Balkan context being "enriched" translated into destruction of the vanquished peoples' civilization, unending misery and degradation for subject Christians and Jews, and eventually, in many places, into their nonexistence. Some enrichment, some appreciation.)

With Bush, demurely wearing their subservient headscarves, were some of the Administration's top female officials, including his then-Homeland Security Advisor, his Deputy National Security Advisor, and Karen Hughes, one of President Bush's closest and oldest *confidantes* and then Assistant Secretary of State for Public Diplomacy. When told that she would not be welcome to visit with Turkish women in Germany, she meekly responded with an offer to send American Muslim women in her place, the beginning of what is touted as a "citizen dialogue" program that sends "Muslim Americans to reach out to Islamic communities across the world." Also note that the "citizen dialogue" is a two-way program, encompassing, for example, an officially sponsored (and U.S. taxpayer-funded) trip to the U.S. of a top-level Kosovo Albanian imam to tour the United States, in cooperation with groups including the notorious Council for American-Islamic Relations (CAIR), to agitate for creation of an independent Muslim Kosovo and urge greater Islamic fidelity among Americans.

Islamophilia is a huge factor in America's Balkan policy. It was in evidence almost two decades ago, in the Administration of George H.W. Bush: in 1992, then Secretary of State Lawrence Eagleburger pointed to the sensitivity of Muslim countries as a guide to the U.S. Bosnian policy. Adopting the Bosnian Muslims as American clients – supplanting the earlier German championing of Croatian interests – even went to the length of cooperating with Iran and al-Qa'ida in providing arms to the Izetbegovic regime.

The same pattern was replicated with our support for the Kosovo Liberation Army. On the question of Kosovo independence, Washington publicly acknowledged the pro-Islamic imperative that drives the policy. At an April 17, 2007, hearing on Kosovo, the late House Foreign Affairs Committee Chairman Tom Lantos (D-CA) called upon "jihadists of all color and hue" to see Kosovo as "yet another example [sic: presumably a reference to Bosnia] that the United States leads the way for the creation of a predominantly Muslim country in the very heart of Europe." At the same hearing, then Under Secretary of State for Political Affairs Nicholas Burns, who was widely seen as one of the main architects of U.S. policy on Kosovo, repeatedly referred not to "Albanians" in Kosovo but simply to "Muslims." Sentiments similar to Mr. Lantos' were expressed in January 2007 by his Senate counterpart, then Foreign Relations Committee Chairman (and current Vice President) Joe Biden (D-DE), who wrote in a *Financial Times* op-ed that Kosovo independence "could yield a victory for Muslim democracy" and "will provide a much-needed example of a successful US-Muslim partnership."

MORE OF THE SAME UNDER OBAMA – One would think, one could at least hope, that after long last the incoming Obama Administration would be able to take a new look at the mistakes of the past and start with a clean slate. If one thought that, or even hoped – one would be wrong. All of the early signals from the new kids on the block indicate that they not only will not repudiate the idiocies of the past, they will intensify them.

First of all, in his inaugural address, Obama promised the Muslim world that America would "extend a hand" – to do what, exactly? Then, after taking office, Obama gave his very first interview to Al-Arabiya, and said: "My job to the Muslim world is to communicate that the Americans are not your enemy...But ultimately, people are going to judge me not by my words but by my actions and my administration's actions."

In her (if you'll pardon the expression) maiden voyage in her now job as Secretary of State, Hillary Clinton declared in her arrival in Jakarta: "If you want to know if Islam, democracy, modernity and women's rights can coexist, go to Indonesia." There are some photos, available on any Google search, of some little Christian girls decapitated by Indonesia proponents of Muslim democracy and modernity Madam Secretary evidently missed.

So far, the Obama Administration's activities directly correspond to several recommendations from the "US-Muslim Engagement Project Report," published in September 2008 through a partnership between Search for Common Ground and Consensus Building Institute. Two of the report's recommendations are to 'elevate diplomacy as the primary tool for resolving key conflicts involving Muslim countries, engaging both allies and adversaries in dialogue' and 'Improve mutual respect and understanding between Americans and Muslims around the world.' "The U.S. has a long way to go in making these recommendations reality," the Report's sponsors say, "but these early trips are a start." Translation: when it comes to crawling before the scowling face of jihad, you ain't seen nuthin' yet.

Finally, as reported by Gulf News, "the mention of a hadith in a speech by Obama that as humans we ought to be guided by the universal truth that no harm should be enacted upon a person that one would not want foisted upon oneself struck a chord in the Muslim world." Evidently the President has a very selective memory from his youthful studies in an Indonesian school (in which, by the way, his religion was listed as Muslim) when it comes to the numerous ahadath and Quranic verses that suggest a very approach to foisting harm on others.

To sum up: the auguries for a change in a policy of appeasement are not good.

There is absolutely no evidence all this pandering has worked. No greater testament to the failure of the policy of pandering to the Islamic world is the 9-11 attack. Having given birth to what later became al-Qa'ida through our mistaken our support for the Afghan mujaheddin – even at that time of dubious wisdom – we compounded our error with our support for Islamic forces in the Balkan. Too little attention has been paid to the numerous references to Bosnia, and several to Kosovo, in the final report of the official, bipartisan U.S. government 9-11 Commission. The Balkans was the essential link in al-Qa'ida's metastasis from an isolated presence in the Hindu Kush into a worldwide menace capable of striking the United States. The Commission's conclusion: a recommendation of more help for Muslims, citing the examples of Bosnia and Kosovo, to impress Islam with our goodwill.

The one-sided phantasmagoria of Serb evil and Muslim innocence concocted by Western governments and media to justify intervention – first in Bosnia and then in Kosovo – far from impressing the Islamic world with our goodwill encouraged an unjustified sense of Muslim victimization. American expectations of reciprocated friendliness display an astounding lack of understanding of the jihadists' mindset. How much "gratitude" did Osama and his boys show for U.S. aid to their anti-Soviet jihad in Afghanistan? In the Balkans, the United States simply reinforced the jihadists' conviction that we were dissolute and weak, and that America was as defeatable as Russia. *See – the* kafirun *are so afraid, they betray themselves one another to us!* Try to find on any Islamic website any indication of Muslim gratitude for Bosnia and Kosovo, which appear instead alongside Afghanistan, Kashmir, Iraq, Chechnya, "Palestine," Mindanao, Xinjiang, etc., in a litany of persecution by an undifferentiated conspiracy of Americans, Russians, Jews, Indians, Chinese, Filipinos, and anybody and everybody else.

Given the imperatives of the post-9/11 world, it is perhaps most incredible that our blinkered Balkans policy even trumps our concerns about internal security. Almost no attention has been paid in the American media to the fact that four of the six defendants in the jihad terror plot to attack Fort Dix in New Jersey are Albanian Muslims from the Kosovo region. The State Department and White House, in their public pronouncements, did everything possible to obscure the Kosovo Albanian origins of the would-be terrorists, encouraging reference to their being from "the former Yugoslavia," perhaps implying they were Serbs. Even less noticed is that the malefactors' presence in the United States – three of them illegal aliens, and one brought to the U.S. by the Clinton Administration as a refugee, another example of Muslim "gratitude" – stems from the fact that a broadly based support network for the Kosovo Liberation Army has been allowed to operate with impunity in the New York-New Jersey-Pennsylvania region, raising funds and collecting weapons, not to mention peddling influence with American politicians.

THE KREMLIN ON THE POTOMAC – A vacuum having been left in European, and even global affairs, at the end of the Cold War, Washington rushed to pick up the pieces left on the board by its former rival. It is often supposed that the drive of the United States to establish itself after the Cold War as the "hyperpower" is based on perceptions of American national interests. Nothing could be farther from the truth. The ideological drive for global hegemony is just that – an ideology without any connection to real national interests. Very few Americans have any real sense of our extended posture in the world and naively accept explanations that our policies are designed to "defend" our nation. Most of the American people have no that we have over a quarter of a million troops in 160 countries around the world, or that our military budget is greater than that of the rest of the world combined! Few Americans are aware that our government funds a vast network of supposed NGOs supposedly promoting "democracy" – let's call it the "Demintern" – but which really use political technologies to bring puppet regimes to power, for example in the so-called "color revolutions" in the former USSR.

The U.S. foreign policy is dominated by a narrow clique of supposed experts, the large majority of whom are dedicated to the proposition that the United States must be the vanguard of all progressive humanity, the midwife of history, brining the rest of the world the only possible enlightened doctrine. These fall generally into the camps of the "liberal interventionists," Democrats like Vice President Biden, Secretary of State Hillary Clinton, and former Secretary of State Madeleine Albright, or, on the Republican side, "neoconservatives" like the late U.N Ambassador Jeanne Kirkpatrick, Condoleezza Rice, and authors of the Iraq war.

The second category, those of the "neoconservatives" in the Republican Party, is especially interesting. The Republicans are generally considered to be the more conservative of the two main U.S. parties. How ironic it is that the foreign policy of this "conservative" party is controlled by a point of view that has its origin in a splinter group from the U.S. Communist Party, and specifically Trotskyite, politics. In this regard, an observation by Russian Foreign Minister Lavrov in 2007 – that U.S. policy struck him as a "replication of the experience of Bolshevism and Trotskyism" – was more on the mark than he could know. "It sounds paradoxical," said Mr. Lavrov, referring to the U.S. attitude toward Russia, "but there was more mutual trust and respect during the Cold War." Or to put it another way, the people now in charge in Washington hate a post-Soviet Russia that is reviving its patriotic and Christian roots more than their predecessors hated communism. A corollary is the expendability of Christians in the Balkans, Kosovo in particular.

Hardly any Americans would know that the top supposedly "conservative" foreign policy gurus are in fact proponents of permanent world revolution. As one prominent and influential advocate of what he called "creative destruction" put it: "We are the one truly revolutionary country in the world."

In the same spirit, Strobe Talbott, a high former official in the Clinton Administration, defined the United States over a decade ago as the embryo of a new global state. "Within the next hundred years," he asserted, "nationhood as we know it will be obsolete; all states will recognize a single, global authority. A phrase briefly fashionable in the mid-20th century – 'citizen of the world' – will have assumed real meaning by the end of the 21st century."

According to Clinton's former Secretary of State Albright, the United States has a special wisdom to use force for good: "If we have to use force, it is because we are America; we are the indispensable nation. We stand tall and we see further than other countries into the future . . ."

This can even mean a reordering of reality itself. According to a prominent jour-nalist's account, who had a meeting with a senior advisor to President Bush in 2002, the advisor told him something that at the time the journalist did not fully comprehend

> *The aide said that guys like me were "in what we call the reality-based community," which he defined as people who "believe that solutions emerge from your judicious study of discernible reality." I nodded and murmured something about enlightenment principles and empiricism. He cut me off. "That's not the way the world really works anymore," he continued. "We're an empire now, and when we act, we create our own reality. And while you're studying that reality – judiciously, as you will – we'll act again, creating other new realities, which you can study too, and that's how things will sort out. We're history's actors . . . and you, all of you, will be left to just study what we do."*

This is the thinking, if we can call it that, behind the U.S. drive to global domi-nance. It is thoroughly un-American: compare the foregoing quotes to the words of George Washington, warning America to preserve its fortunate distance from the af-fairs of other countries and not to enter into supposed alliances – like NATO – that do not serve our own interest: "Why forego the advantages of so peculiar a situation? Why quit our own to stand upon foreign ground? It is our true policy to steer clear of permanent alliances with any portion of the foreign world..."

Even more prophetic are the words of the sixth U.S. president, John Quincy Ad-ams, who seemed even to foresee the current quest for world empire. Two centuries ago he noted approvingly that America "has abstained from interference in the concerns of others, even when conflict has been for principles to which she clings":

> *Wherever the standard of freedom and Independence has been or shall be unfurled, there will her heart, her benedictions and her prayers be. But she goes not abroad, in search of monsters to destroy. She is the well-wisher to the freedom and independence of all. She is the champi-on and vindicator only of her own... She well knows that by once enlist-ing under other banners than her own, . . . the fundamental maxims of her policy would . . . change from liberty to force.... **She might become the dictatress of the world**. She would be no longer the ruler of her own spirit.... [America's] glory is not dominion, but liberty."*

These warning by Washington and Adams reflect the true American principle which our current elite has so crudely violated. In doing so, they have prevented a restoration of a normal political order at the international level and betrayed the welfare of the American people in furtherance of their ideological delirium. In fact, as can be seen in a number of indices, from the U.S. imperial overstretch in Iraq and Afghanistan (where we learned nothing from the Soviet experience, and which President Obama has indicated his intention to repeat in every dismal detail) to the progressive deterioration of the economy, the drive for world domination has cost America dearly.

Can we hope the fever may soon break? It is hard to see how it can continue in the face of the degrading material foundation in the American financial and economic system. For all the overreaching pride and ideological mania that has characterized Washington's drive for world domination, events have inexorably moved in the direction of the failure of that program. The ideologues in Washington have not yet realized that, but they will have to do so as circumstances dictate.

The can be little question that the United States must soon pull back from its imperial ambitions, whether it wants to our not. The question is one of when and how – and how costly the course back home will be. And how much wreckage will be left in her wake.

Finally, as the tide of global empire ebbs, we must all redouble our efforts to ensure that Kosovo is not the last splinter lying on the beach pulled out to sea by the receding waves. The answer to the question of "why Kosovo?" may continue to elude us. The answer to "what must we, all of us, do about Kosovo?" remains clear.

# Racak: The Hoax That Ignited a War

*Julia Gorin*[1]

O January 16, 1999, the Western media went into a fit of rage over the discovery of 45 dead Albanians in the Kosovo village of Racak – allegedly civilians butchered in cold blood by "Milosevic's forces." The head of the OSCE Kosovo Verifying Mission, American diplomat William Walker, immediately asserted that the Serbs were to blame: "From what I saw, I do not hesitate to describe the crime as a massacre, a crime against humanity. Nor do I hesitate to accuse the government security forces of responsibility." Belgrade's claim that the bodies were in fact KLA guerillas fallen during the fight in the surrounding areas was scornfully rejected as "Serbian propaganda." The episode proved to be a key stepping stone to the military attack by NATO two months later.

On January 15, 2009 – the tenth anniversary of "the Racak massacre" – Kosovo's "prime minister" Hashim Thaci and "president" Fatmir Sejdiu awarded the "Gold Medal of Humanity" to Mr. Walker. The leaders used the ceremony, "dedicated to the martyrs of the Racak massacre," to vow "never to forget Serbian crimes."

There could not have been a better tragicomedy roast for the year 2009, the tenth anniversary of NATO's war. The ceremony came nine years after Thaci himself admitted the Racak ploy, a year following its success. Retired Canadian General Lewis MacKenzie, former UN Protection Force commander in Bosnia, cited the former KLA leader's admission in April 2008, in a statement to the Lord Byron Foundation:

---

1 Julia Gorin is a widely published opinion writer specializing in Balkans issues, as well as editor of the humorous book *Clintonisms*.

*[Thaci] has admitted that the KLA orchestrated the infamous Racak "massacre" dressing their KLA dead in civilian clothes, machine gunning them and dumping them in a ditch, and claiming it was a Serbian slaughter of civilians. NATO bought into the ruse and on its 50th birthday, looking for a role in the post-Cold War world, the alliance became the KLA's air force and bombed a sovereign nation from the safety of 10,000 ft.*

Thaci told the BBC in January 1999, "We had a key unit in the region. It was a fierce battle. We regrettably had many victims. But so did the Serbs." He boasted in the same vein but more recklessly in February 2000 to a roomful of foreign correspondents. Most of them dutifully kept a lid on potentially the most sensational story of the decade, leaving only Russian National Radio to report how Hashim Thaci told reporters:

*about the methods of demonizing Serbs, i.e. how his terrorist KLA committed crimes in order to urgently provoke western military intervention in Yugoslavia... [He] admitted that the KLA members killed four Serbian policemen in Racak... Indeed, a police action followed, but it was no punitive expedition of Serb special forces against Albanian farmers, but a legitimate operation against the Albanian extremists who made their stronghold in Racak... In spite of this, NATO and the leading western countries blamed Belgrade for the killing of the so-called Albanian farmers from Racak. That was the first in a series of accusations in an already worked out scenario for deceiving the international public, i.e. preparing the field for the NATO aggression on Yugoslavia.*

A biography of the Finnish forensic scientist Helena Ranta, published in October 2008, revealed that her report on the massacre – which glossed over the true identity of the dead – was coerced. *Helsingin Sanomat* newspaper, whose managing editor authored the book, reported that Ranta said she came under intense official pressure after she was commissioned by the European Union to investigate the events in Racak:

*"Three civil servants of the Ministry for Foreign Affairs expressed wishes by e-mail for more far-reaching conclusions", Ranta said. "I still have the e-mails." ... The investigation by Ranta's working group was very*

*charged from the beginning. It was commonly assumed that Serb forces had perpetrated a massacre... According to Ranta, in the winter of 1999 William Walker, the head of the OSCE Kosovo monitoring mission, broke a pencil in two and threw the pieces at her when she was not willing to use sufficiently strong language about the Serbs.*

Walker continues to claim to this day that it was a massacre and that the Serbs were to blame, "but I never said that; I never made any reference to the perpetrators," the pathologist told the media following her book's publication. "I never said a single word about who stood behind what went on in Racak. That's for the judges to decide, while we forensic scientists just carry out the investigation." She accused Walker of trying to put words into her mouth: "What angered him most was that I refused to use the word 'massacre' and say who stood behind what happened in Racak."

Following the investigation Ranta's full report was not made public. At that time she gave a press conference at which she was vague, admitting there was no evidence of mutilation or torture, and that Yugoslav authorities had cooperated. But she also called the killings 'a crime against humanity,' which was immediately interpreted in the Western media to mean Racak was indeed a cold-blooded massacre.

It is noteworthy that Ranta appeared in 2003 as one of the witnesses in the Hague trial of Slobodan Milošević. She told *Berliner Zeitung* newspaper in 2004 that it was "negative" that a part of the indictment against Milošević was related to the Racak events, based mostly on the version given by Walker. The German daily had obtained access to the complete findings of the Finnish pathologist, and concluded that, "In all probability, there was no Racak massacre at all."

It the immediate aftermath of Racak NATO commander Wesley Clark personally confronted Milosevic with photos of the victims. "This was not a massacre," Milosevic responded. "This was staged."

*The New York Times* reported this exchange on April 18, 1999, three months after it occurred, but failed to add that Milosevic was probably telling the truth. By the time that article was written, serious doubts had been raised about the alleged massacre.

Only days after the "massacre," on January 21, 1999, *Le Monde* noted that William Walker and the Albanians gave the version which raised more questions than it provided answers. "Isn't the massacre of Racak too perfect?" the paper asked.

*How the Serb police could gather a group of men and quietly take them to the place of execution, while they were constantly under the KLA fire? How the ditch at the edge of Racak could escape the glance of the inhabitants, familiar of the places, present before the night? And how come that the observers present for more than two hours in this very small village failed to see the ditch too? Why are there only a few cartridge cases around the corpses, and little blood in this sunken lane where 23 people were supposedly shot several times in the head? Weren't the bodies of the Albanians killed in the combat by the Serb police, and joined together in the ditch to create a scene of horror, in order to initiate the predictable wrath of the public opinion?*

As forensic investigators had subsequently noted, the bodies appear to have been dressed in civilian clothes, then shot additional times and cut with knives several hours after death, in order to simulate a brutal massacre. Nevertheless, Madeleine Albright told CBS's "Face the Nation" that there were "dozens of people with their throats slit" and that the only solution was "humanitarian air strikes."

William Walker was given access to Racak by the KLA while forensic investigators were kept out. Instead of taking steps to secure the alleged crime scene, he brought journalists to the gully and let them trample all over the place. One of the journalists was Franz Josef Hutsch, a German reporter. According Hutsch's subsequent testimony, Walker just stood there while journalists moved the bodies around to take their pictures. He said that the bodies "were put upright, for example, at the edge of the slope so that they would have a bit of shade so that the excessive head wounds wouldn't be seen in a photo to be published. And they were taken from their original positions."

Helena Ranta's ambivalent statements back in 1999 are yet to be openly denied by her today. It is highly revealing, however, that The Hague prosecution removed Racak charges from the indictments against late Yugoslav and Serbian President Slobodan Milosevic, and against the former Serbia's President Milan Milutinovic (who was freed in February 2009) and five other former Yugoslav and Serbian officials.

Five days before beginning airstrikes, Bill Clinton thundered, "We should remember what happened in Racak... innocent men, women and children were taken from their homes to a gully, forced to kneel in the dirt and sprayed with gunfire." The *London Times* was even more imaginative, claiming "that victims had their eyes gouged out, heads smashed in, faces blown away at close range." The victims were supposedly "farmers, workers, villagers, aged 12-74, men, women, children."

Renaud Girard, reporter on the ground for French newspaper *Le Figaro*, described what he saw in very different tones:

> *At dawn intervention forces of the Serbian police encircled and then attacked the village of Racak, known as a bastion of separatist guerrillas. The police didn't seem to have anything to hide, since at 8:30 a.m. they invited a television team (two journalists of AP TV) to film the operation. A warning was also given to the OSCE, which sent two cars with American diplomatic licenses to the scene. The observers spent the whole day posted on a hill where they could watch the village.*
>
> *At 3 p.m., a police communiqué reached the international press center in Pristina announcing that 15 UCK "terrorists" had been killed in combat in Racak and that a large stock of weapons had been seized. At 3:30 p.m., the police forces, followed by the AP TV team, left the village... At 4:40 p.m., a French journalist drove through the village and met three orange OSCE vehicles. The international observers were chatting calmly with three middle-aged Albanians in civilian clothes. They were looking for [possible] civilian casualties. Returning to the village at 6 p.m., the journalist saw the observers taking away two very slightly injured old men and two women.*
>
> *The scene of Albanian corpses in civilian clothes lined up in a ditch which would shock the whole world was not discovered until the next morning, around 9 a.m., by journalists soon followed by OSCE observers. At that time, the village was once again taken over by armed UCK soldiers who led the foreign visitors, as soon as they arrived, toward the supposed massacre site. Around noon, William Walker in person arrived and expressed his indignation.*
>
> *All the Albanian witnesses gave the same version: at midday, the policemen forced their way into homes and separated the women from the men, whom they led to the hilltops to execute them without more ado.*

The pictures filmed by the AP TV journalists – which *Le Figaro* was shown one day before publishing the expose – radically contradicted that version. It was, in fact, an empty village that the police had entered in the morning, sticking close to the walls. The shooting was intense, as they were fired on from UCK trenches dug into the hillside:

> *The fighting intensified sharply on the hilltops above the village. Watching from below, next to the mosque, the AP journalists understood that the UCK guerrillas, encircled, were trying desperately to break out. A score of them in fact succeeded, as the police themselves admitted.*

> *What really happened? During the night, could the UCK have gathered the bodies, in fact killed by Serb bullets, to set up a scene of cold-blooded massacre? A disturbing fact: Saturday morning the journalists found only very few cartridges around the ditch where the massacre supposedly took place... Intelligently, did the UCK seek to turn a military defeat into a political victory?*

It has also been widely noted that, like the ditch itself, the clothing of the dead "civilians" was curiously blood-free. Yet Walker unambiguously declared that the dead "obviously were executed where they lay." His OSCE report spoke of "arbitrary arrests, killings and mutilations of unarmed civilians" at Racak.

None of this threw Western leaders off-schedule:

- NATO announced it was to hold an emergency session the next day "to consider its response to the massacre of more than 40 ethnic Albanians in Kosovo."

- The U.S. State Department declared "there should be no doubt of NATO's resolve." The NATO Secretary-General, Javier Solana, said the alliance would not tolerate a return to all-out fighting and repression in Kosovo.

- The International War Crimes Tribunal on the former Yugoslavia at The Hague announced that it would open an urgent inquiry.

- Secretary of State Albright called Racak the 'galvanizing incident' that meant peace talks at Rambouillet were pointless, and 'humanitarian bombing' the only recourse.

- Germany, which held the presidency of the European Union, said "the international community would not accept such acts of persecution and murder."

- In Paris, the French Foreign Ministry expressed "disgust at the massacre" and called for a meeting of the OSCE to investigate who was responsible.

- UK Foreign Secretary, Robin Cook, said: "Those responsible for the crimes must be held to account before international justice."

- The US special envoy, Richard Holbrooke, condemned the killings, saying they were "the most serious offence since the outbreak of the violence" in the province.

As Mark Ames and Matt Taibbi, currently of *Rolling Stone* magazine, wrote in 1999, Washington responded to Walker's verdict very quickly, setting its military machine in motion, and started sending out menacing invitations to its NATO friends to join the upcoming war party.

> *Walker was in Latin America virtually throughout his entire career, until he arrived in Kosovo. He had no experience in the region which qualified him to head the verification team in Yugoslavia... Walker's role in Racak was to assist the KLA in fabricating a Serb massacre that could be used as an excuse for military action... Eventually, even the Los Angeles Times joined in, running a story entitled "Racak Massacre Questions: Were Atrocities Faked?"*

Ten years of proof that Racak was not a "massacre" went duly unnoticed by Reuters, which on September 30, 2008, published a photo with a caption reading, "The graves of people that were killed by Serbian forces in January 1999 are visited by relatives during the religious holiday of Eid-al-Fitr in the village of Racak, south of the Kosovo capital Pristina."

It is all part of the pattern in which Balkan-Muslim myths from the 90s are perpetuated by media, politicians, military, NGOs, Holocaust museums, filmmakers and artists even while the Muslims themselves admit to the farce. (Upon Karadzic's capture last year, Richard Holbrooke cited "300,000 deaths" in the Bosnian war—three years after Sarajevo's Investigation and Documentation Centre reduced the original inflated figure of 250,000 to less than 100,000.) This is without even questioning why the supposedly secular Balkan Muslims would be visiting the Racak graves on a religious holiday, particularly since the KLA's was a "national" struggle, not a religious one, as we are repeatedly told. U.S. leaders have yet to admit what the KLA themselves have admitted, thereby out-KLAing the KLA itself.

Thaci, meanwhile, has never apologized for the KLA's crimes, while one apology after another is demanded, and extracted, from the Serbian side for what it did and didn't do to counter the terrorist attacks. In fact, the year before the staged Racak massacre—that is, ir, 1998 alone – Thaci killed 40 Serbs and Albanians, including six of his own lieutenants. This, needless to say, was not a green light for the world to bomb Albanians.

Since 1990s Serbian crimes against Albanians, real or imagined, are the basis of the consensus that states Serbia lost all right to Kosovo, by the same token the Albanians who have been terrorizing the province's non-Albanians for the past 10 years (not to mention in preceding decades) should be deemed to have also lost any right to Kosovo.

For his dutifulness William Walker has been rewarded with, among other things, honorary Albanian citizenship. And like Bill Clinton, Bob Dole, Eliot Engel, George W. Bush, and Wesley Clark, Walker has a street named after him in Kosovo. Thus he joins many other KLA members to whom monuments have gone up all over Kosovo. The fruits of his career's crowning mission are still with us in the form of the Kosovo war, now in its eleventh year.

# An observer at a Crow's Court: A Personal Memoir of Kosovo, 1999-2009

*Mary Walsh*[1]

During my years of work in Kosovo I often thought of the stories my father used to tell me about his youth in County Kerry, in the southwest of Ireland. He grew up near Dingle and spent a lot of time up in the Kerry Mountains where he had the opportunity to observe a whole variety of natural phenomena, including – once – a "crow's court."

This is an unusual occurrence, rarely seen but often alluded to in medieval literature. A great congregation of crows surround one unfortunate victim who is the "accused." They isolate the bird and sit on branches around it, preening themselves, with each adopting what appears to be a different role ranging from prosecutor and judge to ordinary court flunkey. For a period it seems like there is a lot of cawing, the crows are busy building the case. Invariably the accused is found guilty and suffers the consequences: the rest of the group descend on the victim and it is pecked to death. Following the "trial" and execution of sentence, the murder of crows (yes, the collective noun is "murder") takes off leaving the battered corpse of the accused to rot.

Nature watchers have never understood this phenomenon: why the group feels the apparent need to pick on one of their own number and then partake in a public, elaborate ceremony, the fatal outcome of which is clearly determined from the beginning.

---

1  Mary Walsh is an Irish international development specialist with ten years' experience on development projects in the Balkans.

One might ask what this has to do with Kosovo. In an analogous way, every-thing.

I landed in Skopje on the evening of the August 23, 1999 and was driven to Pristina the next day. I had no pre-formed views about what was happening in Kosovo, or for that matter in any of part of the former Yugoslavia. I had been planning to work in development in Central America and viewed my assignment in Kosovo as something of an aside, of strictly short-term nature, a few months at most.

The drive from Skopje to Pristina brings to mind the incredible sight of bright yellow sunflowers in the fields on both sides of the road, especially from what I now know to be villages near Lipljan up as far as Laplje Selo and Caglavica. The land on ei-ther side of the road was ablaze with their bright, vibrant colours. What struck me was that, despite the conflict, there seemed to be a lot of farming activity going on. Another memory was the sight of houses burning on either side of the road, small villages in the distance were ablaze and there seemed to be a lot of smoke everywhere. The Albanian driver informed us that these were Albanian villages that had been ethnically cleansed by the Serbs; he informed us that the Serbian army had burned all the houses and he pointed to several villages where allegedly massacres had taken place.

It was not until some time later, when I started working in the area, that I rea-lised that these were actually Serb dwellings in Serb villages, in places like Stari Ka-canik, Grlica, Staro Selo, Talinovac, Srpski Babus and Babljak. Moreover, considering that the Serbian army was forced to withdraw from Kosovo in early June 1999 – some ten weeks earlier – it was hard to see how they could have torched these houses and ethnically cleansed all these villages. Here I was on August 24, more than two months later, looking at burning buildings and destroyed houses that had quite clearly been set on fire only a day or two earlier.

As we approached Pristina I was struck by the number of satellite dishes on the apartment blocks and homes. In briefings prior to my departure I had been led to believe that the ethnic Albanians in Kosovo were poor and deprived, yet this did not tally with the vista as we drove into Pristina. As I got to know Kosovo better, I realized why items such as satellite dishes were a priority. In a province where so many flats and apartments in urban areas were illegally seized and occupied one did not worry about mortgage payments. As I was to discover later, property belonged to those who occu-pied it and not to those who actually owned it. All property was up for grabs.

My early days in Kosovo helped reinforce the sense of the surreal. The town of Pec in the west of the province, where I was based, was the Italian army's area of responsibility. During those days in August I observed in disbelief the sight of these well-tanned, handsome soldiers donning feather be-plumed helmets and sunglasses, often smoking large cigars, as they drove around in heavily armoured vehicles. It was like being on a movie set. It just did not look serious.

My office was located across the road from the UNMIK police car park beside the radio station. Dozens of red and white jeeps – we used to call them the Coca Cola police cars – were parked there, day after day. I could not figure out why they were there for months on end without once moving out. This period, between August 1999 and April 2000, was a time of unprecedented ethnic cleansing – and yet here were these brand new police cars that had made it to a car park in Pec, but got no further than that. Like many other aspects of the international presence in Kosovo, this too was a smokescreen.

The night of September 27, 1999 provided the initial wake-up call for me as to what was going on in Kosovo. I went to bed early with a book while my colleagues went out to have a pizza, about the only thing on offer in those days. I will never forget when the shooting started, it was unremitting. I lay in bed with my head under the covers, disbelieving the scale and intensity of the attacks which went on into the early hours.

That night saw the UCK go on a killing spree, rampaging through the Serb areas of the town, burning, looting and killing mainly elderly Serbs. This all-night rampage happened in a territory where the conflict had officially ended almost four months previously and which had the UN as administrators and police, and which had troops from many Western countries making up the KFOR contingent supposedly to provide security.

The next morning, as I made my way warily down the town, the first thing I saw was a body face down in the river. It was not the only one left lying around the town, but Italian KFOR soldiers had been busy that morning clearing away the bodies. Ironically and not un-coincidentally, the very next day was the deadline for the handover of weapons by the UCK.

I was working on a social development project in Pec. In my first six months I worked only in Albanian villages as that was the area of responsibility designated to us by UNHCR. We were not working in the last Serbian village near Pec to have survived the onslaught after June 1999, Gorazdevac. Furthermore, we were specifically told not to go near that village, and – above all – when driving past it, we were advised not to make eye contact with the Serbs in the village. We were told that the inhabitants of Gorazdevac were thieves and killers and very dangerous as they were all armed. Many times I had been told that they had stolen everything from the Albanians: cars, fridges, televisions, etc. I was warned that if I ever went there I would be raped, beaten and finally murdered.

While most of the internationals believed these scare stories and some tragically enough still do, I found it hard to believe that a village with a church at its centre and with mainly elderly people sitting around the village square could be the evil place that it was made out to be. I first went there in February 2000 as a private individual that is without the 'imprimatur' of my organisation. I travelled in the back of an Italian armed personnel carrier having been told by the soldiers to stay out of sight in the back. What I found there was the exact opposite of what I had been told. People were poor, very poor. Very few people had televisions and there were a lot of elderly women who were in a very difficult situation as they had no accommodation. Despite their difficulties people were very hospitable towards me and on my first day I was offered my first pork meal since leaving Ireland. It was also the first time I ate kajmak and it was delicious.

One of the first projects that I initiated in the village was a social housing project for these women. When I started working there the following month, in March 2000, I encountered great hostility from my colleagues both international and local Albanian. They threatened me, bullied me and one even pushed me down the stairs of our office but I persevered and, then as now, saw nothing wrong in trying to help these poor, unfortunate people who had done nothing wrong to anyone. But what really frightened me was the terrible hatred displayed towards these people, even the look in peoples' eyes when I mentioned I was going to Gorazdevac.

One international colleague who reluctantly helped out on a project which was the rehabilitation of the cultural centre in the village square managed to rehabilitate only half of the roof stating the other half was beyond repair. Later another international NGO completed the roof and their engineer assured me that the other half of the roof was quite easily repairable, stating that from an engineering perspective there was nothing wrong with it and they quickly repaired it. This was the type of blind prejudice that one encountered if one tried to be fair in one's work in Kosovo and especially when a development project for Serb recipients was put forward.

Social exclusion was the order of the day. It was a prejudice that was unrelenting, that led to hatred and ultimately a completely bigoted outlook on the situation in Kosovo. The same colleague who refused to finish the roof later verbally abused me for going to the village to work at weekends (the only way to work there was in my own time at weekends). He stared into my face, screaming at me for working in Gorazdevac. It was the nearest I had ever come to being beaten up.

When villagers wanted to leave Gorazdevac they had only one bus, which was escorted in and out of the village by KFOR. The Serbs were allowed only one bag which was searched repeatedly. The whole setup was as if the powers-that-be wanted deliberately to humiliate these people. As a witness I shared in their humiliation, that ordinary human beings should be treated in such a manner. This was the first time in my life that I had come across people who had no freedom of movement and I could not understand how the people who were holding them hostage and who were rampaging around killing and looting and burning were not subject to any type of restraint.

The hatred against these people, the Serbs, was palpable, intense and shocking to me. There was nothing hidden about it: the hatred was overt and encouraged. This was one of the reasons that I decided to stay on in Kosovo and to try to do something to redress the balance. Out the window went my plans for working in Central America. I had stumbled across a situation in modern Europe, on the eve of the twenty-first century, where there was a systematic denial of basic human rights, where one section of the population had overnight become less than second class citizens – and all this in a place that, theoretically at least, was UN and NATO protection. One question kept coming to mind: how could there be such violations of basic human rights in a UN Protectorate? Who was the UN actually protecting? Who was indicted for repeatedly violating human rights? No one! And when one mentioned the violations and difficult situation of the Serbs, one was threatened and nearly beaten up.

In October 2000 I moved to Pristina to work with an international aid agency. As time went on and as I gathered more experience from my field trips around Kosovo – I had an unfortunate habit of venturing outside the well-controlled "editorial confines" of my office – a different picture from the one we had been led to believe continued to emerge. Gorazdevac was not an exception but the rule. Throughout Kosovo, Serbs and other non-Albanians were suffering similar discrimination. It became increasingly clear to me that international aid in Kosovo from the outset was reserved for those who were judged to be allies of the West and whom the media had branded as the victims. Serbs and other non Albanians were the guilty ones and the international effort in Kosovo clearly followed that line.

Many measures were taken to give the semblance of upholding law and order and justice and human rights; but these, without exception, proved to be part of the smokescreen, the appearance of everything and the substance of nothing. I remember one day meeting the UN regional administrator for Mitrovica outside the UNMIK offices in Pristina who told me that Kosovo would be better off if all the Serbs were gone. I thought that was an amazing statement for any person to make, but especially for a person in his position.

There was a systematic, one might say almost regimented, effort on the part of our Albanian colleagues to present a very one-sided picture, in which the Serbs were quite clearly the culprits and the Albanians the victims. Had I like many internationals stayed in the cocoon of my office relying only on local Albanian sources and western media information, which was rarely more than downright propaganda, I too might have meekly served my time in Kosovo having convinced myself that Kosovo was a black and white issue and that NATO's "humanitarian intervention" was not only justified but was the only way to impose peace and justice.

As the time passed and I stayed in Kosovo longer than I had ever intended, I saw more and more evidence of the campaign of ethnic cleansing. If Albanians or internationals ever mentioned a particular incident, it was usually to condone it saying it was natural that there might be some attacks on the Serbs. There was always a denial, a refusal to acknowledge that an orchestrated, far-reaching campaign going on around us to rid Kosovo of all remaining non-Albanian communities was under way, especially in the urban areas. Even after the concerted and well-organised pogrom of March 2004 which targeted non Albanians throughout Kosovo, the international community maintained its façade of normality and denial, its unspoken campaign of appeasement. I heard people put the 2004 pogrom down to the fact that the Albanian population was "frustrated" which was why mobs destroyed a thousand homes and dozens of churches and displaced over 4,000 people. To this day the Serbs displaced in the March 2004 pogrom are still living in containers (supplied by the Russian government) in Obilic, Gracanica, Uğljare and Kosovo Polje.

Sometimes stories were spread in order to deflect attention away from the real culprits, or to put more blame on the Serbs. They were often ludicrous but they were still passed on and on, especially by internationals who had recently arrived in Kosovo. The electricity supply was poor and there were often blackouts because, the story went, the Serbs did not pay their electricity bills. It did not seem to occur to the people repeating such stories that even if none of the Serbs that remained in Kosovo had paid their utility bills, it was unlikely to account for the drastic electricity shortages endured in the province, given that by October 1999, the Serbs constituted less than 10 percent of the population. Every night I slept in a Serb enclave I went to bed by candle light! It is noteworthy that, prior to June 1999, power cuts were virtually unknown in Kosovo.

Another story doing the rounds was that all the beautiful medieval monasteries and religious sites dotted around Kosovo, for which it is justly famous, were originally

Albanian edifices which had been usurped by the Serbs. One does not have to be an expert in Byzantine religious architecture and art to recognise that the shrines, such as Decani or Pec Patriarchate, were clearly Orthodox in design. The fact that these monasteries were endowments of the Serbian kings given to the Serbian people for posterity was easy to verify.

The claim that the monasteries were originally Albanian was invariably curtailed when I asked the simple question: "If that is so why then do the Albanians keep trying to blow them up?" I never got an answer.

I did not stay safely ensconced in my office, in the company of other internationals who were self-righteously engaged in their anti-Serbian crusade. I travelled to non-Albanian areas, not just Serb areas but also the Roma camps and settlements (such as the lead-contaminated Roma camp in Zvecan for those displaced in 1999 by the UCK in south Mitrovica), the Gorani in Gora, the Croats in Letnica. Since the arrival of KFOR and the UN in Kosovo and the departure of the Serbian security forces, all of them had been on the receiving end of the violence. What ensued in June 1999 and culminated in March 2004 was a war of terror against an innocent civilian population, including Albanians who did not see eye to eye with the UCK and their masters.

This violence was directed solely at civilian targets: men, women and children, regardless of age or infirmity. It was an unremitting war, a war of terror and intimidation intended to drive the non-Albanians out, in some cases aided and abetted by certain contingents of KFOR.

While many Serbian villages were ethnically cleansed, all towns south of the Ibar were cleansed of their Serb and Roma populations. The tales of woe of places like Lipljan, Obilic, Kosovo Polje, Caglavica, Vitina, Urosevac and others are horrendous. The town of Vitina had over 3,500 Serb inhabitants in 1999. A year later there were just a handful left, living huddled around the church. The elderly Serbs in Urosevac were put on buses and taken to the administrative boundary with Serbia-proper, after 1,000 of them had spent nearly a week penned behind a corral in the centre of the town with no facilities. The UCK went on the rampage in the meantime, burning Serbian homes and killing anyone suspected of being a Serb. One UNHCR staff member went to get medicines for them. When she returned she was told that the US army had driven them away in buses to their new homes – collective centres in Bujanovac, in southern Serbia, where many of them still reside. They were the lucky ones: many of those who stayed behind in the villages were tortured, beheaded, raped and murdered.

Despite the sustained assault against them, there were still some Serbs and Roma residing in the town of Obilic by March 2004. They were targeted by the mobs on March 17 of that year as part of the Kosovo-wide drive to cleanse areas south of the Ibar, especially in central Kosovo near Pristina. The international community failed to protect ordinary people. During the attack on Obilic, in which many Serb houses were burned, the entire female population of the Roma settlement in the town – dozens of girls and women of all ages – were stripped naked and marched through the streets by the mob, many of whom were armed. There were soldiers from the British KFOR contingent in the town that day who witnessed the incident but did not intervene. They may have been under orders not to. Whatever the reason, their inactivity was mirrored elsewhere in Kosovo by the inaction of KFOR. They did not turn out to protect those being attacked but in most cases simply stood by and watched. Others scurried off to their bases. There were some exceptions. During the March 2004 pogrom soldiers from the Irish KFOR contingent left their base in Lipljan, acting on their own initiative, and saved the lives of the non-Albanians in Obilic.

An example of the suffering meted out to the innocent is the case of the Nikolic family from Urosevac, whom I am proud to call my friends. Their story stands out as an example of unflagging determination, resilience and courage in the face of frightening odds. Mrs. Dani (Daniela) Nikolic, now in her 80s, was born in Slovenia. She came to Urosevac when she was eighteen to visit her father, an officer in the Yugoslav army. While there she met her husband-to-be; after they were married they settled in Urosevac. Daniela had two daughters, Santipa, and architect, and Liljana, an engineer. The Nikolics were an old, distinguished family in the town. They had contributed much to the development of Urosevac over the years. In 1999 they still owned a part of their large house, the rest of the house was expropriated by the communists.

Their age and inability to be a threat to anyone did not save them from being targeted by the UCK. Although they escaped the initial onslaught against the Serbs in Urosevac, their house was visited many times in June and July 1999 by armed UCK men who stole what they liked. They were all assaulted; all of them had their teeth broken. Santipa was the only able-bodied member of the family; Liljana is a paraplegic due to a car crash some years ago and the mother Daniela is blind. Santipa would venture out to look for food, but was attacked on several occasions and beaten literally black-and-blue. They were protected for some time by Greek KFOR who stationed armed guards at their front door. Despite all the difficulties they stayed in their own house until the March 2004 pogrom, when a mob surrounded the house.

A video tape of the attack on the house survives. It shows that at one end of the town a thousand-strong mob besieged the house of three ladies, while at the other end of town Greek KFOR were trying to defend the church from another mob. Eventually US KFOR came to rescue the Greek contingent, shortly before the interior of the church was torched and some Greek soldiers were badly burnt. US KFOR also came to the Nikolic house and removed the three women who were carried out under a hail of stones and other missiles. Liljana, paralysed from the waist down, was hit on the leg by a rock but did not realise she had sustained a fracture until later. The destruction of their house marked not only the tragedy of losing their family home; it also meant the loss of 18,000 books from their family library, many valuable musical instruments and a priceless work by Giotto of the Blessed Mother. The last vestiges of European civilisation in Urosevac burned with these objects.

The Nikolic ladies were dropped off at the Greek army base where they found other Serb survivors of the final assault on Urosevac. They were not brought to the large US army base at Camp Bondsteel nearby, despite their need for urgent medical attention, because – as it was explained to them later by a US KFOR soldier – US KFOR did not want the local Albanians working on the base to know that they were treating wounded Serbs there. Some ten days later they were brought to Camp Bondsteel for medical attention, but in the meantime one elderly lady had died.

The Nikolic family was returned to the Greek army base in Urosevac where they still reside today – apart from a brief interlude in Greece, where Greek KFOR wanted them to stay. However, the Nikolic ladies did not disappear into the *Nacht und Nebel*. They remain determined to return to their home, although no international – let alone the local Albanian authorities – are anxious to rebuild their house or facilitate their return. In the meantime the house has been completely cut off by new buildings and their access has been denied. The only way for the Nikolic family to visit what remains of their home would be by helicopter. Their father's factory has been "privatised" by the UN-established Kosovo Trust Agency without their knowledge or consent. One soldier told to them recently that the Albanians "deserve" to own the factory as there are so many of them, they are very poor and they need employment. They nevertheless remain determined to stay in their beloved Urosevac.

The simple and stark fact remains that Urosevac, like all the urban centres of Kosovo, is not safe for Serbs to return. The property rights of the displaced count for nothing. No one, international or local, is prepared to stand up for basic human rights. Just ask the elderly Serb refugees from Kosovo accommodated at the collective centre in Kovin, some 80 kilometres north of Belgrade. At lunch time they shuffle up to the canteen to collect their food for the day which they carry in little plastic containers. Their sad faces display the effects of years of incarceration in collective centres, displaced from their homes, robbed of all they own and of all their hopes.

Before I came to Kosovo, although I was not entirely naïve, I had a basic belief in the system of international law and in organisations mandated to uphold and protect justice and human rights. My time in Kosovo opened my eyes to the real workings and infernal machinations of the international system. When I met with a senior representative of the UN Established Returns office in Pristina in February 2005, he quite blatantly told me that Serbs would never be allowed to return to Kosovo. He said that there was no serious intent to facilitate their return and stated that the structures ostensibly established to facilitate their return were nothing more than a smokescreen.

Then there was the British diplomat in Belgrade who self-righteously assured me that "the Serbs were on the wrong side of history." I replied that it must be nice to come from a country that was always on the right side of history. He seemed to miss the ironic note and replied, "Yes, it is!"

The land that I had seen on my first day in August 1999 covered in sunflowers is today a concrete jungle of newly constructed warehouses and buildings, many of which were built illegally. Other plots were sold by Serbs at below the market value simply because they could not continue to live in collective centres and needed the financial resources to move out. Much of the Serbian-owned land away from the road has not been sold but is used illegally by Albanian usurpers.

That the Serbs of Kosovo are being wiped out is beyond dispute. That the eradication of their history and culture is on course is also beyond dispute. The UCK has destroyed most of their churches – 150 in all, including monasteries dating from medieval times. Their graveyards have been desecrated and used as dumps, the bones of their dead desecrated, their villages have been plundered and renamed. Their young have been forced to flee.

My father witnessed a crow's court. I, too, have witnessed it: the murderous crows that I saw ganging up on their helpless victim are the enemies of truth and justice and human rights in Kosovo. The crow in the middle of the court is the Serbian people of Kosovo, on trial for no discernible reason, found guilty in advance, sentenced to death and executed without mercy. The Kosovo situation brings to mind the William Golding novel *Lord of the Flies*, where Piggy is killed by the mob for no reason other than he was different and a scapegoat was needed.

I cannot turn a blind eye to the lethal cruelty of the mob. I cannot turn a blind eye to the supine hypocrisy of those who support and appease the mob to ensure their own "credibility." I will not turn a blind eye to the cruelty of those self-mandated to uphold the law and to resolve conflict in the Balkans, but who sow the seeds of the next war instead.

# The Rambouillet Ultimatum

**Ronald L . Hatchett[1]**

The primary justification for NATO military strikes against the Federal Republic of Yugoslavia in 1999 was its refusal to sign the Kosovo peace agreement put forward by the United States and its allies at Rambouillet, France. President Clinton told us "the Albanians chose peace by signing the agreement even though they did not get everything they wanted." The Serbs, he said, refused to negotiate, even though the agreement left Kosovo as part of Yugoslavia. However, as in several other instances over the lead up to the bombing, the President told us only part of the story.

Most Americans assumed that the deal we offered at Rambouillet was an even-handed one, offering advantage to neither side but addressing the core concerns of Albanians and Serbs alike. Few of us took the time to look at the actual agreement the president condemned the Serbs for not signing. Those who did read the draft saw that the "peace plan" actually gave the Albanians precisely what they wanted: de facto independence immediately, with guaranteed de jure independence within three years.

For the Serbs, signing the Rambouillet agreement would actually have been signing away all Serbian sovereignty over Kosovo. It was not even a "take it or leave it" proposition, as Secretary of State Albright often emphasized back in February 1999; rather, it was "sign it or get bombed." There were, in fact, no negotiations at all, and no sovereign, independent state would have signed the Rambouillet agreement.

---

1 Col. Dr. Ronald L. Hatchett, a former U.S. arms control negotiator based in Vienna, is Professor of international relations at Schreiner University in Texas.

Consider these provisions the Serbs were expected to accept:

- "Kosovo will have a president, prime minister and government, an assembly, its own Supreme Court, constitutional court and other courts."

- "Kosovo will have the authority to make laws not subject to revision by Serbia or the Federal Republic of Yugoslavia, including levying taxes, instituting programs of economic, scientific, technological, regional and social development, conducting foreign relations within its area of responsibility in the same manner as a Republic."

- "Yugoslav army forces will withdraw completely from Kosovo, except for a limited border guard force (active only within a 5 kilometer border zone)."

- "Serb security forces will withdraw completely from Kosovo except for a limited number of border police (active only within a 5 km border zone)."

- "The parties invite NATO to deploy a military force (KFOR), which will be authorized to use necessary force to ensure compliance with the accords."

- "The international community will play a role in ensuring that these provisions are carried out through a Civilian Implementation Mission (CIM) appointed by NATO".

- "The Chief of the CIM has the authority to issue binding directives to the Parties on all important matters he sees fit, including appointing and removing officials and curtailing institutions."

- "Three years after the implementation of the Accords, an international meeting will be convened to determine a mechanism for a final settlement for Kosovo on the basis of the will of the people."

- "NATO personnel shall enjoy, together with their vehicles, vessels, aircraft, and equipment, free and unrestricted passage and unimpeded access throughout the Federal Republic of Yugoslavia (FRY) including associated airspace and territorial waters. This shall include, but not be limited to, the right of bivouac, maneuver, billet and utilization of any areas or facilities as required for support, training, and operations."

- "NATO is granted the use of airports, roads, rails, and ports without payment of fees, duties, dues, tolls, or charges occasioned by mere use."

- "The Parties [i.e. Yugoslavia and "Kosovo"] shall, upon simple request, grant all telecommunications services, including broadcast services, needed for the Operation, as determined by NATO. This shall include the right to utilize such means and services as required to assure full ability to communicate and the right to use all of the electromagnetic spectrum for this purpose, free of cost."

- "In the conduct of the Operation, NATO may need to make improvements or modifications to certain infrastructure in the FRY, such as roads, bridges, tunnels, buildings, and utility systems."

- "NATO shall be immune from all legal process, whether civil, administrative, or criminal."

- "NATO personnel, under all circumstances and at all times, shall be immune from the Parties, jurisdiction in respect of any civil, administrative, criminal or disciplinary offenses which may be committed by them in the FRY."

- "NATO personnel shall be immune from any form of arrest, investigation, or detention by the authorities in the FRY."

The Rambouillet plan gave the Kosovo Albanians total control over the province immediately. It offered them the fruits of victory without the need to fight a war. The only sacrifice required of them was to wait three years before the arrangements were made legally permanent. For the Serbs, the Rambouillet agreement meant that immediately upon signing they lost all sovereignty over Kosovo. Total political control would have been in the hands of the Albanians and the NATO Civilian Implementation Mission. Yugoslav laws would no longer apply in Kosovo. Neither would Yugoslavia be able to exercise police powers in Kosovo. After three years, these arrangements would be made permanent by the "will of the people" – not the people of the whole country of Yugoslavia of which Kosovo is supposedly a part, but only by the will of the people of Kosovo, who are mainly Albanians.

The arrival of NATO troops in Kosovo by itself would have been a gross violation of Yugoslavia's and Serbia's sovereignty. But the requirement that Yugoslavia allow NATO unfettered access to *any and all* parts of the country's territory blatantly violated its sovereignty in so provocative a manner that it cannot have been accidental.

As another commentator has noted, "It is not difficult to imagine a working group in the State Department charged with the task of thinking up the most intrusive and insulting clauses possible to insert into the agreement. Clearly, U.S. policymakers never intended for Yugoslavia's leadership to sign this document." In their book, *Winning Ugly*, Ivo Daalder and Michael O'Hanlon quote a "close aide to Secretary of State Madeleine Albright" saying that the only purpose of Rambouillet was "to get the war started with the Europeans locked in."[2]

The Rambouillet Accord was, in truth, a declaration of war disguised as a peace agreement. The Yugoslav delegation at Rambouillet agreed to give the Albanians autonomy in Kosovo – control over their day-to-day lives including religious, education and health care systems, and local government operations. But they tried to negotiate changes to preserve the right of the Yugoslav federal government to determine economic and foreign policy, for Yugoslav national law to continue to apply in Kosovo, and for any international presence in Kosovo to be limited to observation and advice, not control. The Serbian negotiating efforts were summarily dismissed and the Serbs were told they had only two choices: sign the agreement as written or face NATO bombing.

When the conflict ended after 78 days of bombing, Yugoslavia remained in control of Kosovo. Serbian military losses were few. A combination of weather, cunning, and low-tech diversions confounded NATO's multibillion dollar high-tech weapons, as they tried to find and destroy Serbian military targets in Kosovo. A US Air Force after action report obtained by *Newsweek* said NATO verifiably destroyed just fourteen Serb tanks, eighteen armored personnel carriers, and twenty artillery pieces.[3]

So why did Yugoslavia agree to terms to end the fighting? NATO offered both carrots and sticks. The sticks were onerous – and many would say, illegal. Frustrated by lack of success in rooting out the Serb military, NATO shifted the bombing focus to civilian infrastructure targets in Serbia – electrical power grids, petroleum refineries and storage areas, automobile manufacturing plants, heating plants for Belgrade residential high rises, even tobacco factories. At the same time, however, NATO supported a joint EU-Russian effort to broker an end to the conflict which appeared to offer important concessions to the Serbs.

EU emissary, Martti Ahtisaari of Finland, and Russian emissary Viktor Chernomyrdin put forward a plan that essentially superseded the Rambouillet ultimatum. The details, subsequently incorporated in *UNSCR 1244 Principles for Kosovo Peace,* eliminated the demand for NATO forces to have access to all Yugoslav territory. It also provided for Kosovo to remain a part of Yugoslavia and for Yugoslav control over Kosovo borders and Serbian cultural sites there. The Kosovo Albanians were to have autonomy

---

2  Ivo Daalder and Michael O'Hanlon, *Winning Ugly: NATO's War to Save Kosovo.*Brookings Institution, 2000.

3  *The New York Times*, April 17, 2000; *Newsweek*, May 15, 2000

but not independence and an international force and civilian administration under the UN, not NATO, would oversee return of refugees. Had this type of agreement been offered at Rambouillet, the tragedy of "the Kosovo war" might have been avoided.

Unfortunately the UNSC 1244 provisions were never fully implemented. Yugoslav security forces were never allowed to take up positions on the frontiers of Kosovo or at Serbian cultural sites. A European Union Rule of Law Mission in Kosovo, (EULEX Kosovo) eventually replaced the UN administration envisaged by the United Nations Security Council Resolution 1244, although Russia and Serbia initially considered the EU mission illegal. Albanian ethnic cleansing attacks against Serb and other non-Albanian groups were unchecked by the EU-led forces. During the years of international control, over 200,000 non-Albanians in Kosovo were driven from their homes. In March 2004 ethnic Albanians took part in a three-day wave of attacks on Serbs and other minorities, as well as on UN buildings and property. 19 people were killed and 4,000 forced from their homes; 34 historic Christian churches and monasteries were destroyed.

Despite this record of violence the EU encouraged the Albanians to unilaterally declare independence and on June 15, 2009, turned over power to a new Kosovo Albanian government. The new "country" is hardy an example of political, economic and social success. After nine years as an international protectorate and billions of dollars in aid and reconstruction funds, its economic prospects are grim. Unemployment is 57 percent, and among youths it is closer to 70 percent; half the population is under 25. The World Bank estimates that 37 percent of the population lives on less than $1.75 a day. Organized crime is big business: drugs, prostitution, guns. Non-Albanians have been herded into smaller and smaller enclaves.

Still, EU nations, with the exception of Spain, Slovakia, Greece, Cyprus and Romania, recognized the Albanian government as did the United States. Russia, China, India, and a host of countries in South America, Africa and Asia have not done so. International opposition to the unilaterally proclaimed Kosovo state is primarily based on the precedent it sets. Many states have areas within their borders where a minority of the overall national population is the majority; for example Catalonia and the Basque region in Spain, the Hungarian area of Transylvania in Romania, Tibet in China, Chechnya in Russia, and Sikh and Moslem- majority areas in India.

The history of NATO actions in Kosovo makes nations with restless minorities fear that the NATO juggernaut might turn its attention to aiding the "liberation" of minorities within their borders who strike out at the legitimate government and then cry oppression when the government cracks down on their violence. It is clear that

NATO countries did not think through the long term implications their actions in Kosovo could have in their own countries. Does the United States really want to establish an international norm that would call for California to accept the independence of San Diego and Los Angeles counties if the Hispanic majority there decides to break away? Will the U.S. accept the secession of a Hispanic –dominated Texas or New Mexico? France, an independent Corsica or Brittany? The answer is, "of course not."

The reality is the NATO action in Kosovo was not motivated by high goals such as humanitarianism or supporting self-determination for national minorities. The Kosovo action was the use of naked power in an attempt to impose a government in a sovereign country more consistent with the political objectives, economic interests and cultural outlook of the dominant NATO partners, especially the United States.

# The Debate on NATO's Ground War

Jürgen Elsässer[1]

In early June 1999 Prime Minister Tony Blair of Britain, the most outspoken advocate of a ground invasion of Kosovo, had ordered the preparation of 30,000 letters calling up Britain's army reserves. As was revealed by *The New York Times* six months after the event, "Typed and addressed, they were about to go into the mail, making possible the commitment of up to 50,000 British troops – half the standing army – to go into Kosovo." In Washington, the same source says, President Clinton was about to give his own approval to preparations for a ground invasion of Kosovo, including up to 120,000 American troops – despite his vow, in a televised speech on the first day of the war, March 24, that "'I do not intend to put our troops in Kosovo to fight a war.'"

At almost the same time, former Prime Minister Viktor S. Chernomyrdin of Russia and President Martti Ahtisaari of Finland were in Belgrade, laying out NATO's terms to Mr. Milosevic, but few in Washington expected Milosevic to agree to them.

It is only now, a decade after the event, that we know the extent to which an all-out ground war against Serbia was considered as a viable option by NATO planners. Had that option prevailed, the death toll would have been incomparably greater.

The extent to which German officials were toying with this idea can be deduced from what Joschka Fischer, former minister of foreign affairs, said nine months after

1 Journalist and political analyst Jürgen Elsässer is an author specializing in geopolitics, terrorism and the Balkan wars. This article is an updated segment from his recent book *Kriegslügen. Der NATO-Angriff auf Jugoslawien* (Berlin, 2008).

the war, when asked why Milosevic had agreed to the ceasefire. He was coerced by the bombs, Fischer replied, by Russia's influence, and by "the awareness of the ground offensive to come... which he knew he would lose."[2] In his memoirs, however, Fischer tries to make the impression that German troops would not have taken part in the invasion, since a majority in the Bundestag authorizing such action had never seemed even remotely likely.[3]

By contrast, Fischer's biographer Michael Schwelien is of the opinion that the German government was even more aggressive on the issue than the United States: "While Chancellor Gerhard Schröder blithely held out the prospect of ground troops even before the air strikes had started, U.S. President Bill Clinton wanted none of that."[4]

German efforts to initiate a ground war could be observed as early as summer 1998, under the previous government. The coalition of Social Democrats and the Green Party went on kindling with the so called Extraction Force. Consisting of 1.700 NATO soldiers, this force was standing ready for battle by the borders of F.R. Yugoslavia, first October 1998 in the FYR of Macedonia, later in Albania, too, allegedly to secure the withdrawal of OSCE observers.

When the tensions tightened up after the Racak incident in January 1999, NATO institutions and the German Bundestag discussed an enlargement of the mission. The ministry of defense stated that it is "quite possible to deploy the Extraction Force" if the crisis escalates.[5] *Frankfurter Allgemeine Zeitung* announced that "Government [is] ready to send troops to Kosovo."[6] Schröder had explained that he was unwilling to exclude the possibility that Germany would "within and together with the community of states" send ground forces into "non-pacified areas."[7] Defense minister Rudolf Scharping swung the moral whip when he declared, "It is not the time for ultimatums any more, but for mere action. We will not watch people being slaughtered."[8] Roland Friedrich, the chronicler of the German Association for Foreign Policy, sums up the German role: "Being the first NATO member country to officially advance the idea of offensive military strike [against Yugoslavia], Germany yet again was a pioneer, very similar to the situation in May 1998, when Klaus Kinkel exerted the pressure."[9]

2 Michael Schwelien, Joschka Fischer. Eine Karriere, Hamburg 200, S. 106/107.

3 Joschka Fischer, Die rot-grünen Jahre. Deutsche Außenpolitik – von Kosovo bis zum 11. September, Köln 2007, S. 206.

4 Michael Schwelien, a.a.O., S.105.

5 Roland Friedrich, Die deutsche Außenpolitik im Kosovo-Konflikt, Wiesbaden b2005, S.69.

6 FAZ 23.01.1999.

7 Heinz Loquai (German General at OSCE Headquarter in Vienna), *Weichenstellung für einen Krieg. Internationales Krisenmanagement und die OSZE im Kosovo-Konflikt*, Baden-Baden 2003, S. 117.

8 FAZ 23.01.1999.

9 Roland Friedrich, a.a.O., S. 69.

German conservatives were more moderate, unlike in the summer before. After the war had started Edmund Stoiber (former CSU chairman), Volker Rühe (former minister of defense) and Freidbert Pflügler came out in opposition to the war.[10]

When the withdrawal of OSCE observers was completed on March 20, 1999, the Extraction Force – supposedly established to protect them – nevertheless remained *in situ*. In early May 1999 the controversy about their mission reached another climax. In his memoirs, Fischer remembers that "the 'ground offensive' option menacingly started to push itself more and more into the foreground."[11] This is hardly surprising since NATO air strikes had remained ineffective, despite the increase in the number of daily bomber missions from 50 to 300 since May 6. That number was to peak at 500 by the end of war.[12] Despite all of NATO's public claims that the Yugoslav army was being badly hurt, NATO generals understood that the army was well dug in and was not going to be bombed out of Kosovo. Increasingly, therefore, NATO strikes were aimed at putting political pressure on Milosevic and his government by bombing civilian targets like bridges, roads, heating plants and electrical power stations.

The crucial debate on preparing a ground invasion is likely to have taken place on May 28 among five defense ministers of the leading NATO states. Experts see this as he best documented secret meeting of the whole conflict. Who demanded the invasion? Who resisted it?

Even authors with access to official files give differing answers. Günter Joetze, expert of the German Foreign Ministry, reports that Clinton's National Security Advisor Sandy Berger aimed for a ground offensive without Germany, a "coalition of the willing." Italy, France and Great Britain supposedly had already agreed on supporting the United States.

Roland Friedrich, however, advocated "utter restraint" in Rome and Paris on this issue. Even greater controversy surrounds Scharping's attitude on May 28. According to author Tim Judah, the German did not oppose the invasion at all; Ivo H. Daalder and Michael E. O'Hanlon write that especially "Germany and the U.S. remained unyielding."[13]

On the other hand, contemporary witnesses from the German Ministry of Defense assured Friedrich that Scharping and his officials were "strictly" against any

---

10 Günter Joetze, *Der letzte Krieg in Europa. Das Kosovo und die deutsche Politik*, Stuttgart / München 2001, S. 132.

11 Joschka Fischer, a.a.O., S.208.

12 vgl. Günter Joetze, a.a.O., S. 130.

13 Tim Judah, *War and Revenge*. Suffolk 2000, S. 270f.; Ivo H. Daalder / Michel E. Hanlon, *Winning Ugly. NATO's War to save Kosovo*, Washington 2000, S. 158.

ground offensive from the very beginning.[14] This was conveyed to Joetze, too: "In every debate in the second half of May Schröder said that Germany would participate in the air strikes to the end, but that a ground offensive was out of question."[15]

The only available authorized source is Rudolf Scharping's war log in which he barely touches the issue, referring to its "top secret" status. Yet what little he tells us is quite revealing:

> *"Moreover, and with a view to consultations within the G8, we wanted the troops, declared to NATO as a guarantee of political result, to be stationed instantly."[16]*

This sentence is so confusing as to be hardly intelligible. One thing is clear: in addition to the Extraction Force, NATO troops were to be deployed in the war theater, allegedly to secure a political solution.

Such a "solution" was not even remotely on the horizon on May 28, however. Quite the contrary: the previous day the International Criminal Tribunal for the former Yugoslavia announced its indictment against Slobodan Milosevic. This example of ICTY's upfront co-operation with NATO indicates that no key player on the Western side wanted to negotiate with Milosevic at that moment, and that nobody was seriously looking for a political solution.

"'We knew he would have to capitulate sometime," one senior Western official told *The New York Times* when it was all over. "The only question was when. And no one expected him to cave in so soon."

Milosevic's eventual acceptance of NATO's terms surprised the Western powers on June 3. Russian support for NATO's terms may have played a role in his decision, as well as the prospect of more intensive air strikes against Belgrade's bridges and electrical and water systems. Nevertheless, the hints that a ground invasion was imminent are likely to have impacted Milosevic more than other considerations. In addition, he had won some important diplomatic shifts in NATO's stand. Important from his point of view, it was the United Nations that would – at least formally – sanction the peace and control Kosovo, rather than NATO, and Kosovo was acknowledged, for the time being at least, to be a sovereign part of Yugoslavia.

---

14  Roland Friedrich, a.a.O., S. 116.
15  Günter Joetze, a.a.O., S. 132.
16  quoted in Michael Schwelien, a.a.O., S. 104/105.

# U.S. Policy and Geopolitics of Jihad: The Green Corridor in the Balkans

**Srdja Trifkovic**[1]

The *Green Transverse* or "Green Corridor" (in Serbian/Croatian: *Zelena transverzala*[2]) is a geopolitical concept that has been used in two distinct, albeit interconnected meanings:

1. To define the long-term goal of Islamist ideologues, both in the Balkans and in the wider Muslim world, to create a geographically contiguous chain of majority-Muslim or Muslim-dominated polities that will extend from Turkey in the southeast to the northwestern-most point of Bosnia (120 miles from Austria).[3]

---

1 Dr. Srdja Trifkovic, for many years foreign affairs editor of *Chronicles*, is Executive Director of The Lord Byron Foundation for Balkan Studies.

2 The term "Zelena transverzala" first gained prominence 25 years ago, just before the Winter Olympics in Sarajevo in 1984. The organizing committee – dominated by Bosnian Muslim members of the Communist Party ("League of Communists," SKJ) – decided to give the sports hall built for the event an unusual name, "Zetra." This was the acronym for the Green Corridor (ZElena-TRAnsverzala); it supposedly referred to the belt of urban parkland in central Sarajevo. Some observers – including Bosnian anti-terrorism expert Dzevad Galijasevic, himself a Muslim – believe that the choice of the name was anything but incidental.

3 In a 2001 report by the Italian security services, the *dorsale verde* is defined as "the project of Islamic colonization of the Balkans that aims at the gradual establishment of a green corridor to include all regions in which predominantly Muslim ethnic groups prevail." Cf. Fiorenza Saranzini: "Soldi e moschee, Osama avanza nei Balcani." *Corriere della Sera*, November 8, 2001, p. 11. See also "Come nasce la *dorsale verde*" in *Limes*, 3/1998, pp. 15-27.

2. To denote the ongoing process of increasing ethno-religious self-assertiveness among major traditionally Muslim communities in the Balkans,[4] this has had a four-fold effect:

(a) Expanding the geographic area of their demographic dominance;

(b) Establishing and/or expanding various entities under Muslim political control with actual or potential claim to sovereign statehood;

(c) Enhancing the dominant community's Islamic character and identity within those entities, with the parallel decrease of presence and power of non-Muslim groups; and

(d) Prompting Muslim communities' ambitions for ever bolder designs in the future, even at the risk of conflict with their non-Muslim neighbors.

Giving some clarity to this concept is essential to a comprehensive understanding of the motives, actions, and emerging expectations of different actors in the Yugoslav wars in general and the ongoing Kosovo crisis in particular.

**Reality Denied** – Political, cultural, religious and demographic trends among Muslim communities in the Balkans strongly suggest that the Green Corridor is taking shape, either deliberately or spontaneously.[5] Nevertheless, many Western academic experts and media commentators (especially in the English-speaking world) have shown the tendency to be *a priori* dismissive of any suggestion that a long-term Islamic geopolitical design exists in the Balkans, let alone that it is being deliberately and systematically pursued. The notion of the Green Corridor was thus criticized as a product of Serbian propaganda with "Islamophobic" overtones, although its most authoritative proponents have been institutions and experts with no ethnic or personal axe to grind in the Balkan imbroglio.

The Bosnian war was still raging when Sir Alfred Sherman, former advisor to Prime Minister Margaret Thatcher and co-founder of The Lord Byron Foundation, warned that the Muslims' objective was "to create a 'Green Corridor' from Bosnia through the Sanjak to Kosovo" that would separate Serbia from Montenegro.[6] Western powers are "in effect fostering this Islamistan," Sherman warned, and developing "close working relations with Iran, whose rulers are keen to establish a European base for their politico-religious activities." In addition, "Washington is keen on involving its

---

4  Massimo Nava, "Il nostro Afghanistan", in *Limes Quaderni Speciali* 4/2001, pp. 177-185.

5  Cf. Laura Iucci: "La Bosnia resta un serbatoio di terroristi." *Limes* (Rome), No 6-2003, pp. 203-208.

6  Sir Alfred Sher.nan: "Let's Remove the Blinkers." *The Jewish Chronicle*, September 30, 1994.

NATO ally Turkey, which has been moving away from Ataturk's secularist and Western stance back to a more Ottomanist, pan-Muslim orientation, and is actively helping the Muslim forces."

"Jihadist Network in the Balkans" from the Italian geopolitical review *Limes* (October 2008) shows the western half of the Green Corridor (*La dorsale verde*) and key centers of Islamic activity

Sherman's diagnosis proved to be prescient. A decade later it was echoed by Col. Shaul Shay of BESA Center at Bar-Ilan University. He noted that "the Balkans serve as a forefront on European soil for Islamic terror organizations, which exploit this area to promote their activities in Western Europe, and other focal points worldwide." His verdict regarding the Green Corridor is disquieting:

> *[T]he establishment of an independent Islamic territory including Bosnia, Kosovo and Albania... is one of the most prominent achievements of Islam since the siege of Vienna in 1683. Islamic penetration into Europe through the Balkans is one of the main achievements of Islam in the twentieth century.*[7]

7 Shaul Shay, *Islamic Terror and the Balkans.* Transaction Publishers, 2008.

Shay's account shows how the Bosnian war provided the historical opportunity for radical Islam to penetrate the Balkans at a time when the Muslim world – headed by Iran and the various Islamic terror organizations, including al-Qaeda – came to the aid of the Muslims. The Jihadist operational-organizational infrastructure was thus established.

John Schindler, professor of strategy at the U.S. Naval War College and former National Security Agency analyst and counterintelligence officer, concurs: in his view the Balkans provide the missing piece in the puzzle of al-Qa'ida's transformation from an isolated fighting force into a lethal global threat.[8] Radical Islam played a key role in the Yugoslav conflict, Schindler says: like Afghanistan in the 1980s, Bosnia in the 1990s became a training ground for the mujahidin, leading to blowback of epic proportions.

The Green Corridor paradigm reflects Samuel Huntington's *Clash of Civilizations,* which used the war in Bosnia and Herzegovina as a paradigmatic case of the so called "fault-line wars" between Islam and the rest. Many years before the first shots were fired in Bosnia in 1992, that paradigm was confirmed by Alija Izetbegovic. In his *Islamic Declaration* Izetbegovic denied any chance of "peace or coexistence between the Islamic faith and non-Islamic societies and political institutions":

> *"Islam contains the principle of ummet, the tendency to unite all Muslims into a single community – a spiritual, cultural and political community... It is a natural function of the Islamic order to gather all Muslims and Muslim communities throughout the world into one."*[9]

During the Bosnian war (1992-1995) Izetbegovic presented a "pluralist" image to the West, but his followers acted in accordance with his primary message. The fruits of their labor – and that of their coreligionists in another half-dozen countries in the region – are clearly visible along a thousand miles' trail through the middle of today's Balkans.

**Ottoman Legacy** – Unlike other European peninsular regions (Iberia, Italy), the northern boundary of the Balkans is not marked by mountain ranges. That boundary is open and crossed by several key transit corridors connecting Central and Western Europe with the Middle East and eastern Mediterranean. This has been the bane of the region's history, inviting invaders and turning the Balkans for most of the modern era into an object of competing designs and interests of outside powers.

---

8   John R. Schindler, *Unholy Terror: Bosnia, Al-Qa'ida, and the Rise of Global Jihad.* Zenith Press, 2007.

9   Alija Izetbegovic, *Islamska deklaracija.* Sarajevo: Mala muslimanska biblioteka, 1990.

The Ottoman conquest and occupation left an indelible mark on the region. It started in 1354, when Ottoman Turks crossed the Dardanelles from Asia Minor and established a foothold on the northern shore. The subsequent spread of Islam in the Balkans was "by the sword": it was contingent upon the extent of Ottoman rule and the establishment of political and social institutions based on the teaching of Kuran and the Islamic legal and political practice. The line of the attack went from Thrace via Macedonia to Kosovo; through the Sanjak into Bosnia all the way to the Una River, was finally stopped at the Habsburgs' Military Frontier created in the 16th century.

It is noteworthy that *the geographic thrust of the Ottoman attack and later colonization of Muslims from other parts of the Empire in the Balkans coincided exactly with the "Green Corridor."* From earliest days the Green Corridor has had a geopolitical logic that influences political and military decision-making. Furthermore, Ottoman efforts at Islamization of the local population were more determined, and more successful, along the "Corridor" axis (Thrace-Macedonia-Kosovo-Sanjak-Bosnia) than in other conquered Christian lands (e.g. in mainland Greece, central Serbia, northern Bulgaria, or Wallachia).

The Ottoman conquest destroyed the materially and culturally rich Christian civilization of Byzantium and its dynamic and creative Slavic offspring in Serbia and Bulgaria. *The conquered populations became second-class citizens* ("dhimmis"), whose physical security was predicated upon their abject obedience to the Muslim masters.[10] They were heavily taxed (*jizya*, or poll tax, and *kharaj*) and subjected to the practice of *devshirme*: the annual "blood levy" (introduced in the 1350s) of a fifth of all Christian boys in the conquered lands.

Conversion to Islam, a phenomenon more strongly pronounced along the Green Route than in the central regions of the Empire, was near-universal among northern Albanians, including the settlers in Kosovo. This contributed to a new stratification of the society under Ottoman rule and a new power balance. It favored local converts to Islam, eager to assert their power over their former co-religionists, Christian *gaiurs*. This resulted in far harsher treatment of their Christian subjects than was mandated from the Porte, and helped ignite uprisings in Serbia (1804) and Greece (1821). The 19th century witnessed a more thorough oppression of the Christian communities under Ottoman rule than at any prior period.

At the same time, some great powers (Great Britain in particular) supported the continued Turkish subjugation of Balkan Christians on the grounds that the Ottoman

---

10 "The attitude of the Muslims toward the Christians and the Jews is that of a master toward slaves," a British diplomat, H.E.W. Young, reported as late as 1909, "whom he treats with a certain lordly tolerance so long as they keep their place. Any sign of pretension to equality is promptly repressed."

Empire was a "stabilizing force." France's and Britain's alliance with Turkey against Russia in the Crimean War (1853-1856) reflected a frame of mind and a strategic calculus – the desire to score points in the Muslim world vis-à-vis another, non-Muslim power – that has manifested itself in recent years in the overt or covert support by those same powers for the Muslim side in Bosnia and Kosovo, and somewhat less overtly in the Israeli-Arab conflict.

**Demography** – The most enduring, politically and culturally relevant consequence of the Ottoman rule in the Balkans is the presence of large indigenous Muslim communities. The Balkan Peninsula is one of the most ethnically and religiously diverse regions in the world, especially considering its relatively small area (just over 200,000 square miles) and population (around 55 million).[11] Of that number, Eastern Orthodox Christians – mainly Greeks, Bulgars, Serbs and Slavic Macedonians – have the slim majority of around 53 percent; Sunni Muslims (11 million Turks in European Turkey and a similar number of Albanians, Slavic Muslims and ethnic Turks elsewhere) make up 40 percent; and Roman Catholics (mainly Croats) are at around 5 percent.[12]

Those communities do not live in multicultural harmony. Their mutual lack of trust that occasionally turns into violence is a lasting fruit of the Turkish rule. Four salient features of the Ottoman state were institutionalized, religiously justified discrimination of non-Muslims; personal insecurity; tenuous coexistence of ethnicities and creeds without intermixing; and the absence of unifying state ideology or supra-denominational source of loyalty. It was a Hobbesian world, and it bred a befitting mindset: the zero-sum-game approach to politics, in which one side's gain is perceived as another's loss. That mindset has not changed, almost a century since the disintegration of the Empire.

Most Balkan Muslims live in continuous swathes of territory along the Green Corridor. There are but two major gaps in the chain. One is in northeastern Macedonia, where 80 miles divides easternmost Albanian villages near Kumanovo from the westernmost Bulgarian-Muslim (i.e. Pomak) villages in the Bulgarian southwestern corner at Blagoevgrad. The other is in the region of Raska (northern Sanjak) in southwestern Serbia, along the main road and railway from Belgrade to Montenegro.

The Christian communities all over the Balkans are in a steep, long-term demographic decline. Fertility rate is below replacement level in every majority-Christian

---

11 All data based on official statistics, adjusted for Panonian (non-Balkan) regions of Serbia and Croatia.

12 The region's once-thriving Jewish community was destroyed during World War II, with the enthusiastic participation cf two Waffen SS divisions, *Hanjar* (Bosnian-Muslim) and *Skenderbey* (Kosovo-Albanian).

country in the region.[13] The Muslims, by contrast, have the highest birth rates in Europe, with the Albanians topping the chart. On current form it is likely that Muslims will reach a simple majority in the Balkans within a generation.

**The Role of Modern Turkey** – Turkey's European foothold is populous (over 11 million) and overwhelmingly mono-ethnic (Turkish) and mono-religious (Muslim); the Christian remnant is negligible. A nation-state of 72 million, the Turkish Republic is based on a blend of European-style nationalism and an Islamic ethos that breeds a sense of intense kinship with the Muslim communities further west in the Balkans.

The Kemalist dream had never penetrated beyond the military and a narrow stratum of urban elite. For decades described as the key to U.S. strategy in eastern Mediterranean, in the Middle East, and—more recently—in the oil-rich Caspian region and the sensitive ex-Soviet Central Asia, the country is ruled by the ever more openly Islamist *Justice and Development Party* (AKP) of Prime Minister Recep Tayyip Erdogan. The AKP "espouses an ideology of cultural divide, tension, and conflict, despite all of the pro-Europe rhetoric in which Islamists in Turkey engage in their pursuit to exploit the European Union for their agenda of Islamization."[14] That agenda is no longer confined to the borders of the Turkish state. There is a rekindled sense of kinship among the growing ranks of Turkish Islamists with their Balkan co-religionists and with the old Ottoman domains further west. The re-Islamization and assertiveness of Turkey under Erdogan is essential to the revival of Islam and ethnic self-assertiveness all along the Green Corridor:

> *The [Yugoslav] wars of the 90s opened whole areas where they [Muslims] were in the majority: While the regional realities modified, so did geopolitics between those who remained in their traditional homes in the Balkans and the ever expanding Islam over Europe itself [with] pan-European Islamic clusters from the West southward into the Balkans themselves. Of the utmost importance to Muslims in Western Europe, but especially the Balkans, is the admission of Turkey into the EU, for Ankara will be a voice for all Muslims inside the E.U. itself.*[15]

Without a strong, solidly supportive anchor at its southeastern end, no Muslim revival in former Ottoman lands along the Balkan Green Corridor would be possible. The mix of nationalism and Islamism in Turkey aims not only at reversing the process

---

13  It now stand at -0.83 percent in both Bulgaria and Greece.

14  Bassam Tibi, "Turkey's Islamist Danger." *Middle East Quarterly*, Winter 2009.

15  "The Role of the Balkan Muslims in the Shaping of Europe," *Muslim Media Network*, May 4, 2008.

of modernization of the past 85 years; it also aims at reversing the outcome of the pre-ceding period of Ottoman decline. Under the AKP Turkey is becoming increasingly revisionist, potentially irredentist, and detrimental to stability in the Balkans.

**Bulgaria** – Of the country's 8 million inhabitants, ethnic Turks account for just under ten percent (750,000). Southern Bulgaria is also home to several hundred thousand Pomaks, Islamized Slavic speakers. Their number is unknown as they are not recognized as a distinct ethnic group: officially they are "Muslim Bulgarians."

Most Pomaks and Turks live in six districts that connect Turkey with FRY Macedonia: Haskovo, Kardjali, Smolian, Blagoevgrad, and southern parts of Pazard-zhik and Plovdiv. The Pomaks are experiencing an intense Islamic religious revival, mainly financed from the Arab world. Hundreds of new mosques have been built in recent years. Middle Eastern "charities" are also establishing Kuranic schools, paying for trips to the Hajj, and offering scholarships to young Pomaks to study Islam in Saudi Arabia. Since religion defines their identity, "these poor, pastoralist Slavic Muslims have become prime targets for Arab proselytizers seeking to make inroads in Bulgaria, the EU country with the largest indigenous Muslim population."[16]

In addition to the religious revival, the Pomaks are establishing a new form of ethnic identity.[17] Some Pomak activists assert that, far from being "Islamized Bulgar-ians," they are descended from ancient Thracians.[18] Others assert Arab descent and an Islamic identity that antedates Turkish conquest. Many Bulgarians see such assertions as the first step in a future call for the establishment of a Pomak state – Islamic in char-acter – in the Rhodope region as the key link to the Western Balkans. Some politi-cians warn of "unprecedented aggression based on religious and ethnic grounds" and accuse Muslim activists of "contempt for the laws of the Republic of Bulgaria."[19] Even pro-Western sources in Sofia concede that "it is stretching credibility to 'imagine" that Bulgaria is not a target of radical Islam.[20]

**Former Yugoslav Republic of Macedonia** – FYROM is widely considered the weakest state in the Balkans. Macedonian Slavs account for 66 percent (1.3 million) and Albanians for 25 percent (500,000) of the republic's two million people. The lat-ter, 98 percent Muslim, have had a remarkable rate of growth since 1961, when they

---

16  Christopher Deliso, *The Coming Balkan Caliphate*. Praeger, 2007, p. 106.

17  In November 2008 the "Justice Federation," a Pomak NGO in the town of Gotse Delchev, declared hat Pomaks were separate ethnicity and demanded their own TV channel and political party.

18  This claim is similar to the Albanian assertion of "Illyrian" descent: by implication, Ortho-dox Christian Slavs (Serbs, Bulgarians) are the relative "newcomers," whose claim to the land is therefore more tenuous.

19  FOCUS News Agency, January 10, 2009: www.focus-fen.net/index.php?id=n166573.

20  Clive Leviyev-Sawyer, "Radical Islam in Bulgaria?" *The Sofia Echo*, April 16, 2007.

accounted for 13 percent of the total. Albanian birthrate is more than twice that of the Slavs. Following the signing of the Ohrid Agreement that ended the 2001 armed rebellion by the "NLA" (a KLA subsidiary); the state itself is effectively becoming bi-national and bilingual. Albanians are *de facto* the second constituent nation in FY-ROM. They are guaranteed proportional share of government power and ethnically-based police force.

Having secured their dominance along the borders of Albania and Kosovo, the current main thrust of the Albanian ethno-religious encroachment has the country's capital city as its primary objective. It is a little-known fact that today's Skopje is effectively as divided as Nicosia, or Jerusalem, or Mostar. Once a city quarter becomes majority-Albanian, it is quickly emptied of non-Albanian (i.e. Slavic-Macedonian, non-Muslim) population. The time-tested technique is to construct a mosque in a mixed area, to broadcast prayer calls at full blast five times a day, and to create the visible and audible impression of dominance that intimidates non-Muslims ("sonic cleansing"). In those mosques a Wahhabi-connected imam or administrator is invariably present to keep an eye on the rest.[21] Through their links with Arab donors they can influence the payment of salaries to imams and administrative staff.

During the 2001 Albanian rebellion the NLA was largely financed by the smuggling of narcotics from Turkey and Afghanistan, but in addition to drug money, "the NLA also has another prominent venture capitalist: Osama bin Laden."[22] French terrorism expert Claude Moniquet estimated in 2006 that up to a hundred fundamentalists, "dangerous and linked to terrorist organizations," were active or dormant but ready in sleeper-cells in Macedonia. New recruits are offered stipends to study Islam in Saudi Arabia, and they are given regular salaries and free housing to spread the Wahhabi word on their return to Macedonia.[23]

Both demographically and politically, the Republic of Macedonia has a precarious present and an uncertain future. In the aftermath of Kosovo's unilateral declaration of independence, FYROM's long term stability and sustainability are open to doubt.

**Kosovo** – Former U.S. Ambassador to the United Nations John Bolton warned in early 2008 that "Kosovo will be a weak state susceptible to radical Islamist influence from outside the region... a potential gate for radicalism to enter Europe," a stepping stone toward an anti-Christian, anti-American "Eurabia."[24] His was a rare voice in Washington to warn of the ongoing merger of aggressive greater-Albanian nationalism

---

21  Deliso, op. cit., p. 84.
22  The Washington Times, June 22, 2001.
23  "Fissures in Balkan Islam," *The Christian Science Monitor*, February 14, 2006.
24  Voice of America interview, February 17, 2008.

and transnational Islamism. Bolton's verdict is shared by former UN commander in Bosnia, Canadian Gen. Lewis McKenzie. In 1999 the West intervened "on the side of an extremist, militant Kosovo-Albanian independence movement," he says. "The fact that the KLA was universally designated a terrorist organization supported by al-Qaeda was conveniently ignored."[25]

Since the 1999 US-led NATO intervention, Kosovo has become the crime capital of Europe.[26] Crime is the province's main economic activity: hard drugs (primarily heroin), followed by human trafficking, associated sex trade, and arms smuggling.[27] But no less significant, from the vantage point of the Green Corridor, has been the symbiosis that has developed between Kosovo's Albanian crime families and the Jihadist networks abroad. As a result, according to a 252-page report compiled by U.S. intelligence agencies in April 2006, Islamic militants have been freely crisscrossing the Balkans for more than 15 years: "extremists, financed in part with cash from narcotics smuggling operations, were trying to infiltrate Western Europe from Afghanistan and points farther east via a corridor through Turkey, Kosovo and Albania."[28]

This process started well before the 1999 NATO intervention, but the Clinton Administration ignored the warnings.[29] The relationship was cemented by the zeal of KLA veterans who joined Bin Laden's network in Afghanistan.[30] Iran also supported the Albanian insurgency in Kosovo, hoping "to turn the region into their main base for Islamic armed activity in Europe."[31] By the end of 1998 U.S. DEA officials complained that the transformation of the KLA from terrorists into freedom fighters hampered their ability to stem the flow of Albanian-peddled heroin into America.[32]

By that time the NATO bombing of Serbia was in full swing, however, and the mujaheddin were, once again, American "allies."

A decade later Kosovo is run by those "allies." It is the worst administered and most corrupt spot in Europe,[33] a mono-ethnic hotbed of criminality and intolerance,

---

25 Lewis Mackenzie, "We Bombed the Wrong Side in Kosovo." *The National Post,* April 6, 2004.

26 Less than a year after NATO intervention, on 10 March 2000, the UN human rights rapporteur Jiri Dienstbier dec'ared that "Kosovo is in chaos," having become "a mafia paradise." Reuters, 20 March 2000.

27 Cf. Norbert Spinrath, president of the Association of German Police Officers, in *Der Spiegel,* December 15, 1999. In March 2008, a similar picture was presented in a report by the UN Office on Drugs and Crime.

28 "Terrorists use Balkan corridor." *International Herald Tribune,* April 18, 2006.

29 *The Jerusalem Post,* September 14, 1998.

30 *USA Today,* November 26, 2001.

31 *The Sunday Times* (London), March 22, 1998.

32 *The Washington Times,* May 4, 1999.

33 In a November 2008 progress report, the European Union said "corruption is still widespread and remains a major problem in Kosovo… due to insufficient legislative and implementing measures."

a major source of irredentism and regional instability – and a key pillar of the Green Corridor.

**Sanjak** – The region known to Muslims as Sandžak ("administrative district" in Turkish) is one of the most critical geopolitical pressure points in the Balkans. It covers some 8,500 sq.km. along the border between Serbia and Montenegro, linking Kosovo to the southeast with Bosnia to the northwest. Bosniaks and Muslims-by-nationality accounted for 52 percent while Serbs and Montenegrins had 43 percent, with smaller groups making up the balance. The crucial demographic gap in the Green Corridor exists in the northwestern half of Sanjak, comprising three municipalities in Serbia (Priboj, Nova Varos and Prijepolje) and Pljevlja in Montenegro. If there is to be a fresh crisis in the Balkans over the next decade, it is to be feared that this will be its location.

After Montenegro proclaimed independence in May 2006, the Muslim demand for autonomy is focused on the six municipalities on the northern side of the border, in Serbia. Such an entity would have a 58% overall Muslim majority. More importantly, even in the reduced format it would still provide the all-critical land bridge between Kosovo and Bosnia.

**Bosnia** – Alija Izetbegovic's memorable assertion in his *Islamic Declaration* that "there can be no peace or coexistence between the Islamic faith and non-Islamic societies and political institutions," and that his goal is "a great Islamic federation spreading from Morocco to Indonesia," was not unusual for a sincere Islamist.[34]

Bill Clinton was still in the White House when a classified State Department report warned that the Muslim-controlled parts of Bosnia were a safe haven for Islamic terrorism.[35] This was confirmed in November 2001 when Bosnian passports were found in a house in Kabul used by the fleeing Taliban.[36] The core of Bin Laden's Balkan network consists of the veterans of El Moujahed brigade of the Bosnian-Muslim army. The unit was distinguished by its spectacular cruelty, including decapitation of prisoners to the chants of *Allahu-akbar*.[37]

After the end of the Bosnian war, many Muslim volunteers remained.[38] The Bosnian-Muslim government circumvented the Dayton rules by granting them Bos-

---

34 Cf. Lieutenant Colonel John E. Sray, USA, *Selling the Bosnia Myth to America: Buyer Beware*. U.S. Army Foreign Military Studies Office, Fort Leavenworth, KS, October 1995.

35 *The Los Angeles Times*, October 7, 2001.

36 AP, November 21, 2001.

37 Videos of such gruesome spectacles are circulated through Islamic centers and Internet sites in the West.

38 *The Washington Post*, November 30, 1995.

nian citizenship.[39] The Bosnian veterans went on to perpetrate murder and mayhem in many countries in Europe, North Africa, the Middle East, Asia, and North America.[40] They planned the Millennium Plot and the bombing of the Al Khobar building in Riyadh.[41] They plotted to blow up U.S. military installations in Germany.[42] Even 9/11 itself had a Bosnian Connection: Khalid Sheikh Muhammad, who planned the 9/11 attacks, was a seasoned veteran of the Bosnian jihad, as were two of the hijackers.[43]

As *Jane's Intelligence Review* concluded in 2006, "The current threat of terrorism in Bosnia and Herzegovina comes from a younger, post-war generation of militant Islamists, radicalized by US actions in Iraq and Afghanistan."

**The Green Corridor and the War on Terrorism** – In the Balkans, a phenomenon initially based on local groups is morphing into an integral part of a global network. Al-Qaeda and its loosely linked Balkan offshoots, or self-starting independent cells merely inspired by it, are capable of fielding operatives who are European in appearance and seemingly integrated into the Western society – the "white al-Qa'eda."[44] Western law-enforcement officials concede that the region has become "a paradise" for Islamic radicals."[45]

By contrast, Western politicians and diplomats are typically evasive. They do not deny the existence of the problem, but tend to relativize it by adding that it is unlikely to disturb the political and security balance in the region, or to damage Western interests. As a former diplomat notes, "Then usually follows the reassuring mantra about the pro-European orientation of secularized Balkan Muslims with the optimistic conclusion that the accelerated process of the Euro-integration of the whole region would narrow tne space for radical Islamism until such tendencies will finally disappear."[46]

A major fault of the Western approach is its naïve faith in the attractive powers of secularisation. There is a growing gap between the reality of Islam in the Balkans and Western mainstream narrative about the allegedly moderate and tolerant "Balkan Islam." The problem of the Green Corridor will not be resolved without critical reex-

---

39 "Mujaheddin Remaining in Bosnia," *The Washington Post*, July 8, 1996.

40 "Le troisième membre du 'gang de Roubaix' se revendique proche du FIS." *Le Monde,* October 6, 2001.

41 *The New York Times*, June 26, 1997.

42 The Los Angeles Times, October 7, 2001.

43 John Schindler, author of *Unholy Terror*, in *World Magazine*, Vol. 22, No. 35, September 27, 2007.

44 "Terrorist Cells Find Foothold in the Balkans," The Washington Post, December 1, 2005.

45 Gregory Katz, "Terrorists said to be getting aid in Balkans," *Houston Chronicle*, December 27, 2005.

46 *Chronicles Online*, April 6, 2006. www.chroniclesmagazine.org.

amination of Western policies as well as Western illusions. That problem has morphed over the past two decades into a demographic, social and political reality:

> *"[W]hile the Muslims have established a continuity which drives a wedge within Christian Central Europe, the West is looking with indifference at that evolving situation which they hope will create a docile, Turkish-like Islam. But in view of the trouble Turkey itself is suffering from Muslim fundamentalists, it is doubtful whether these hopes will be fulfilled."[47]*

The U.S. policy in Southeast Europe over the past two decades in general, and Washington's Kosovo policy in particular, have had the effect, by design or default, to favor the aspirations of various supposedly pro-Western Muslim communities in the Balkans along the geographic line extending from Turkey north-westwards towards Central Europe.[48] That policy was based on the expectation that satisfying Muslim ambitions in a secondary theater will improve the U.S. standing in the Muslim world as a whole.

The policy has never yielded any dividends, but repeated failure only prompts its advocates to redouble their efforts. Former U.S. Under-Secretary of State Nicholas Burns thus declared on February 18, 2008, a day after Kosovo's unilateral declaration of independence: "Kosovo is going to be a vastly majority Muslim state, given the fact that 92 to 94 percent of their population is Muslim, and we think it is a very positive step that this Muslim state, Muslim majority state, has been created today. It's a stable – we think it's going to be a stable state."

If it is intrinsically "a very positive step" for the United States that a "vastly Muslim state" is created on European soil that had been "cleansed" of non-Muslims then it should be expected that Washington will be equally supportive of an independent Sanjak that would connect Kosovo with Bosnia, of a centralized, i.e. Muslim-controlled Bosnia that will abolish the legacy of Dayton, or of any other putative Islamistan in the region – from yet-to-be federalized Macedonia to a revived Eastern Rumelia in southern Bulgaria. It is worthy of note that the Organization of the Islamic Conference statement, to which the State Department referred so approvingly, announced that the Islamic Umma wishes its brothers and sisters in Kosovo success: "There is no doubt

---

47  Raphael Israeli: *From Bosnia To Kosovo: The Re-Islamization Of The Balkans*. Ariel Center for Policy Research, Policy Paper No. 109, 2004.

48  Cf. a "programmatic" article on the U.S.-sponsored Greater Middle East by two *New Republic* editors, Jacob Heilbrunn and Michael Lind: "The Third American Empire." *The New York Times*, January 2, 1996.

that the independence of Kosovo will be an asset to the Muslim world and further enhance the joint Islamic action."[49]

"There is no doubt," indeed. Far from providing a model of pro-Western "moderate Islam," Kosovo, Muslim Bosnia, Sanjak, western Macedonia, and southern Bulgaria are already the breeding ground for thousands of young hard-line Islamists. Their dedication is honed in thousands of newly-built, mostly foreign-financed mosques and Islamic centers. The intent was stated by the head of the Islamic establishment in Sarajevo. "The small jihad is now finished ... The Bosnian state is intact. But now we have to fight a bigger, second jihad," Mustafa Ceric, the Reis-ul-Ulema in Bosnia-Herzegovina, declared over a decade ago. This statement reflects the inherent dynamism of political Islam: a truce with Dar al-Harb is allowed, sometimes even mandated, but a permanent peace is impossible for as long as there is a single infidel entity refusing to submit to Dar al-Islam.

If Western and especially U.S. policy in the Balkans was not meant to facilitate the Green Corridor, the issue is not *why* but *how* its effects paradoxically coincided with the regional objectives of those same Islamists who confront America in other parts of the world. Far from enhancing peace and regional stability, such policies continue to encourage seven distinct but interconnected trends centered on the Green Corridor:

(e) Pan-Islamic agitation for the completion of an uninterrupted Transverse by linking its as yet unconnected segments.

(f) Destabilization of Bosnia resulting from constant Muslim demands for the erosion of all constitutional prerogatives leading to the abolition of the Republika Srpska.

(g) Growing separatism among Muslims in the Raska region of Serbia, manifest in the demand for the establishment of an "autonomous" Sanjak region.

(h) Continuing intensification of greater-Albanian aspirations against Macedonia, Montenegro, Greece, and rump-Serbia.

(i) Further religious radicalization and ethnic redefinition of Muslims in Bulgaria, leading to demands for territorial autonomy in the Rhodope region.

(j) Ongoing spread of Islamic agitation, mainly foreign-financed, through a growing network of mosques, Islamic centers, NGOs and "charities" all along the Route.

---

49  Ekmeleddin Ihsanoglu, the head of the OIC, as quoted by Reuters, February 19, 2008.

(k) Escalation of Turkey's regional ambitions and Ankara's quiet encouragement of all of the above trends and phenomena.

In all cases the immediate bill will be paid by the people of the Balkans, as it is already being paid by Kosovo's disappearing Serbs; but long-term costs of the Green Corridor will haunt the West. By encouraging its Albanian clients go ahead with the UDI, the U.S. administration has made a massive leap into the unknown. That leap is potentially on par with Austria's July 1914 ultimatum to Serbia. The fruits will be equally bitter. While their exact size and taste are hard to predict right now, that in the fullness of time both America and Europe will come to regret the criminal folly of their current leaders is certain. Pandora's Box is wide open.

# Serbia, Israel, and the Islamic Challenge

*Raphael Israeli*[1]

Numerous comparisons have been made between the seemingly parallel situations concerning Serbia-Kosovo-Albania on the one hand, and Israel-Jordan-Palestinians on the other. Some elaboration is in order that would put this intriguing matter to rest. Such comparisons are often resorted to by both sides of the divide, invoking strikingly resembling narratives and mirror-image arguments to justify each party's cause. Remarkably similar moulds of development have been evolving, which evinces once again the validity of the old adage, *plus ça change, plus c'est la même chose.*

Two independent ethnic-majority states, Israel and Serbia, are the anchors of the regional controversy in their respective areas, where ethnicity and faith are intertwined: Israeli Jewishness and Serbian Orthodoxy. Both treasure a long history of separate existence and of hard-won, constantly challenged, defended and painfully maintained independence. Adjacent to them, the persistent existence of independent nation-states of Albania and Jordan, respectively, each harboring an ethnic-religious-national entity of their own (Palestinians and Albanians, respectively), not necessarily friendly to their neighbors; and maintaining living family, social, cultural, historical, political, economic and linguistic ties with their kin in territories of their neighbors – the West Bank and Kosovo, which are precisely considered as the historical heartlands of Israel and Serbia.

---

1 Dr. Raphael Israeli, historian and Islamologist, is Professor at the Hebrew University in Jerusalem and a fellow of the Truman Institute for Peace.

What is more, both countries have also been the home to a considerable and growing minority in its territory proper – Palestinians in Israel (inadequately dubbed the Israeli Arabs) and Albanians in southern Serbia. And just as diaspora Palestinians are dispersed in the neighboring and western countries, so does one encounter Albanians in Macedonia, Montenegro, Western Europe and the US.

**Settlements and their Erosion** – Apart from the perennial challenge of dealing with a restive and mostly hostile minority at home, both Israel and Serbia have also had to tackle their relations with their immediate neighbors.

The Arab-Israeli wars since 1948, and the breakup up of Yugoslavia which coincided with the end of the cold war and the collapse of Communism and the Soviet bloc, have contributed to instability on the borders of these two states. Their constant vacillations have been in accordance with the fortunes of those wars, which resulted in the intervention of outside powers to restore stability. In Israel, following the peace process between Israel and Egypt in the 1970's, the Oslo peace initiative was launched in the 1990's to seek a settlement with the Palestinians that would also insure Israel's security.

The Serbs, after the Dayton peace settlement on Bosnia which was negotiated (imposed) by the Americans in 1995, thought that their territorial integrity was guaranteed, and attempted to concoct a new formula for keeping together the remnants of Yugoslavia (Serbia with Kosovo and Montenegro).

Both hoped-for settlements were geared to bring permanent tranquility to Israel and Serbia, both admittedly at a territorial price, but without prejudice to the security or territorial sovereignty of either. Following Oslo (1993), which envisaged a degree of Israeli withdrawal from the West Bank as part of a permanent settlement with the Palestinians, Israel and Jordan rushed to normalize relations in a peace treaty (1994). This is where Jordan and Albania differ. Albania became the champion of Albanian minorities in the Balkans outside its sovereign territory and stirred unrest among the Albanians of Serbia (ever since 1968) and Macedonia (during the civil war of the turn of the millennium), and aided its kin across its borders with other states. Jordan, by contrast, cut itself off the West Bank and contented itself with the special status it was accorded by Israel in Jerusalem under the terms of the peace treaty.

The commonality of Palestinian nationhood was not affected by this exercise. They picked up the role which was abdicated by Jordan, and began to promote it. It is as if Albania had changed its name and were recognized by the world as Tirania (and its citizens as Tiranians), and its Albanian identity and claim to statehood were taken over by the Albanians of Kosovo, who – because seemingly stateless, since Albania had vanished – were entitled to world support, under the sacrosanct rule of self-determination, for independence and statehood. The absurdity of the situation in Kosovo is that the West has been endorsing its claim to a second Albanian state at the expense of Serbia's sovereignty, while it is prevailing on the Jewish state to allow a second Palestinian state – in addition to Jordan – at the expense of Israel's security and sovereignty.

After the bombing of Serbia by NATO in 1999, the international forces and the UN administration in Kosovo were supposed to protect both the territorial integrity of Serbia and the survival of the Serbian population in Kosovo, together with its historical, religious and cultural heritage there. But it did nothing to prevent the utter destruction of that heritage and the systematic ethnic cleansing of the Serbs who were relegated to a persecuted, frightened and waning minority. In the West Bank, the Oslo Accords submitted the places of Jewish heritage to "guaranteed" Palestinian Authority protection, but when the Intifada broke out in 2000, both the Joseph Tomb in Nablus and the Jewish synagogue in Jericho were burned down by the Palestinians, while the PA forces of public order looked on.

The UN administration was supposed to ensure that before the status of Kosovo was discussed, standards were to be enforced on guaranteeing the security and right of the Serbs. But soon erosion set in, when standards and status were lumped together in one go, as the international administration failed to make one the prerequisite of the other, as required, and then it ended up adopting the status of independent Kosovo without any standards discussed or attained. So much for international guarantees.

That is no more than a replay of the Oslo Accords and then the infamous "Road Map." In Oslo, the Palestinians undertook first to put an end to terror and violence as a legitimate way to tackle their problems with Israel. But as soon as they were repatriated from their Tunisian exile and handed power and weapons, they reverted to terror. They learned that those who use violence end up gaining; being the weak side of the equation entitles them to blind support from abroad regardless of what they do.

**Claims and Disclaimers** – In this manner weakness became the major strength of both the Albanians and the Palestinians. Serbs were bombed and ousted from their country, which was ceded to the imposters who invaded it, under the watching eye of the West. Israel was applauded by the West when it gave up territory out of its own volition, in the hope of bringing the Palestinians to terms, but when the latter's intransigence grew instead; they found that the support of the West for them did not abate. The Palestinians rapidly learned that they can bomb Israelis indiscriminately, pester their lives and terrorize them with impunity, because as soon as something was done to arrest their aggression, they immediately posed as the victims and hurled accusations of "horrors", "genocide", "holocaust", "Nazism", "war crimes" and the rest against the defenders, who were so demonized as to make any calumny against them appear excusable. That exact same scenario was repeated during the Gaza War of 2009, in the aftermath of which Israel is still shelled, but it cannot react forcefully without arousing the wrath of the world which does not suffer the consequences of that aggression.

Retrace the events in Kosovo since the start of the crisis, and you detect the same stages, tactics and stratagems played out by the Albanians and Palestinians respectively, and the international community, with few exceptions, aligning itself with the weak and the victim who was also the imposter and the aggressor. Why would the West do that? Why would the Christian world relinquish its natural and tested allies, who constitute the backbone of its geo-strategic security and shoot itself in the foot by boosting the forces inimical to it, which in the long run are bound to precipitate its demise?

By catering to Muslim demands and Muslim causes, like the Palestinian and Kosovo issues, the West hopes to appease the "moderate" Muslim regimes, like Saudi Arabia, Pakistan, Algeria, Jordan, Morocco, Kuwait and Egypt, and perpetuate the flow of oil which has become the lifeline of the industrialized world.

American foreign policy, which was followed by the rest of NATO members, was to attract through alliances and economic development the emerging Muslim nations of Central Asia and the Balkans to the Turkish model and to create a continuum of *moderate Islam* from the confines of China through Pakistan and Central Asia, to Turkey and the newly constituted entity of Bosnia-Herzegovina. The US wished not only to maintain intact the borders of the former Yugoslav republics, but also to ensure the continuity of the majority-Muslim Bosnia as part of the grand scheme of the Muslim "moderate" continuum. But when the Albanians in FYR Macedonia rebelled to demand a greater share of power, the West prevailed on the weak Macedonians to appease the Albanians. Kosovo Albanians then rose to violate the very principle of territorial integrity that America so vehemently defended in Dayton, and allowed them to terrorize the Serbs and force them out of their land, thus appeasing the Muslims once again.

But, as usual, what the Americans had envisaged is not what they achieved after they made all the possible mistakes. Turkey has turned itself fundamentalist Muslim in 2002 and refused thereafter to accommodate the American strategic needs in Iraq. Bosnia, under Alija Izetbegovic, made connections to Iran and Chechnya, not to the liking of the US, and the "Kosovars" – at least that part of the KLA which was ideologically committed to Islamic revolution – do not seem to follow the Western blueprint. The Christian continuum, which used to connect Russian Orthodoxy via central

Europe down to Serbia and Greece to the Aegean Sea, has been disrupted as the Muslim wedges – Bosnia, Kosovo, Macedonia, possibly the Sanjak – have been driven into the heart of Europe. In Bosnia and Herzegovina itself, reports abound of an intense Wahhabi activity, and of inflammatory fundamentalist rhetoric by Saudi-sponsored Imams, who have rendered the Western dream of moderate Islam in the Balkans into a sad and dangerous joke.

**The Futility of "Constructive Ambiguities"** – One of Henry Kissinger's lessons of diplomacy to the world has been his theory of "constructive ambiguities", namely than when two unbridgeable positions make agreement impossible, one is advised to find the formula which provides that bridge by enabling each of the parties to interpret it to his liking. While that formula may have had some temporary benefits to it, when the day of reckoning came and the formula had to be applied to the real world, it turned out that there was no agreement; the discrepancies burst out in earnest. Security Council Resolutions, which say one thing and its reverse, are spectacular "masterpieces" which illustrate the point.

The campaign to Islamize Palestine and Kosovo, undertaken by Muslim interests and supported by a West that is steeped in ambivalent approaches and ambiguous formulae, has come to its crucial defining stage: Will the West rethink its position, reconsider who are its friends and foes, align with the former and stand firmly against the latter, and turn to construct a solid wall of the Western civilized world again the new wave of barbarians which is determined to vanquish it and reduce it to *dhimmitude*?

Palestine and Kosovo must be seen in the context of the third invasion of Islam into Europe. The first invasion in the 8th century had taken Europe by assault from the southwest, colonized the Iberian Peninsula and attempted to take over Gallic France until it was arrested by Charles Martel in 732. The Spanish *reconquista* which took centuries to reclaim that land, was not completed before the end of the 15th century, at the very same time that the second invasion of the Ottomans, this time from the southeast, swept through the Balkans and eventually made headway to the gates of Vienna.

The retrieval of the lands once ruled by Islam (Andalusia, Palestine, the Balkans and Kashmir) is a matter of the highest priority from the Islamic point of view. Attacking India or the European Union by Islam outright is too risky. Therefore attention is centered on the easier targets of Palestine and the Balkans, with Andalusia, Sicily and Kashmir in the second stage. For the rest of Europe a new tactic of soft invasion, by immigration and demographic explosion, has already yielded impressive results: within one generation, 30 million Muslims have taken a foothold in Europe.

The active help the disciples of the Prophet receive from the West in the Balkans is an Allah-sent bonus that they had never dreamt of. The declaration Kosovo's "independence" in early 2008, which was recognized by the United States and most West Europeans, has been the most dramatic manifestation of this Western capitulation in the face of Islamic aggression in the heart of Europe. At the same time, the Hamas and Hizbullah, backed by Iran and encouraged by the Muslim successes in the Balkans, continue to press in Palestine. Their fellow jihadists are active in Kashmir, too.

The threat is for the most part unstated, but clear: if the West does not accommodate Islam by exacting more concessions from India and Israel – as it did in the Balkans – both the Arab states and Pakistan may succumb to the fundamentalists. The West seems to be losing its nerve and all its bearings. It is falling into the trap of Islamist extortion, thereby precipitating itself swiftly onto the sliding path into the precipice.

# The "Fools' Crusade" Continues

**Diana Johnstone[1]**

The 1999 war against Yugoslavia opened a new phase of history. It amounted to a new declaration of independence by the United States – independence from both international law and the restraint on its military action exercised by the counter-power of the Soviet Union. The United States could thus begin a conquest of the world.

This is not an exaggeration; it was heralded by Bush senior as the New World Order – the same term used by Nazi Germany in relation to Europe.

The American conquest is not to be carried out with the bluster of Mussolini or the racist raving of Hitler. The style is different, the causes and purposes are different, but many of the procedures and results are similar.

The ethnic conflicts in Yugoslavia were used as the pretext to release the United States from the restraints of the post-World War system. As usual in such cases, the pretext was moral: a vast propaganda campaign portrayed the conflicts in Yugoslav, which had complex economic, historic and political causes, as a simple instance of good versus evil. The Serbs were evil, likened to the Nazis and Hitler. Non-Serbs were virtuous victims. The "International Community", the prevailing euphemism for the Great Powers led by the United States, were said to be morally obliged to act militarily to save the innocent victims from evil Serbs.

---

1  Dr. Johnstone is an author specializing in European affairs. Her books include The Politics of Euromissiles (Verso, London, 1983) and Fools' Crusade: Yugoslavia, NATO and Western Delusions (Pluto Press/Monthly Review 2002).

An endless series of lies, distortions and omissions were necessary to establish that simplistic version of events in public consciousness. Many of us have exposed those lies over and over, but they continue to flourish as vigorously as ever. Here I shall skip over that seemingly futile exercise.

No matter who did what to whom, the Yugoslav conflicts were deliberately exploited and exacerbated in order to stage a little war that NATO was sure to win "out of area", beyond the defense perimeter of the Atlantic Alliance. This initiated a new era in which the United States could drag Western Europe into an enterprise of world conquest. Of course, it is never called "world conquest". Sometimes it is called "humanitarian intervention", sometimes it is called "the war on terror", and sometimes it is merely "ensuring stability"or "promoting democracy" or "regime change."

There are always new "threats" to be met by the "International Community" – energy access, cyber war, rogue states, failed states, and of course "genocide." But if you examine it carefully, what is going on is a project for world conquest. It probably will not succeed – such projects rarely succeed – but that is what it is.

### Causes and Effects of US Wars

How and why is the United States pursuing world conquest? My first answer is that the how and the why are the same thing. I don't believe that a scheme has been cooked up in some capitalist headquarters, say at Bilderberg. This is neither a conspiracy nor a nationalist movement. There is no impassioned nationalist orator exhorting the American people to take over the world. Indeed the majority of American people care very little for the rest of the world. They probably don't want it. No, this world conquest is primarily a matter of institutional inertia.

In January 1961, in his farewell speech as he left the Presidency, General Dwight D. Eisenhower warned of the "military-industrial complex".

> *In the councils of government, we must guard against the acquisition of unwarranted influence, whether sought or unsought, by the military-industrial complex. The potential for the disastrous rise of misplaced power exists and will persist. [...] Only an alert and knowledgeable citizenry can compel the proper meshing of the huge industrial and military machinery of defense with our peaceful methods and goals so that security and liberty may prosper together.*

Eisenhower did not suggest dismantling the military-industrial complex. He only called on "an alert and knowledgeable citizenry" to keep it from getting out of hand. Well, an "alert and knowledgeable citizenry" has been asleep at the switch for about half a century.

The original expression was "the military-industrial-congressional complex," but Eisenhower decided to let Congress off the hook. Nevertheless, Congress is an essential part of the whole complex, because members of Congress vote regularly for military appropriations to benefit their constituencies. Prodded by industrial backers, Congress even votes for weapons systems the Pentagon hasn't asked for and doesn't know what to do with. That is the pork barrel system that keeps military spending soaring and more and more weapons being researched, developed and built. Thus the people's elected representatives are part of a socio-economic system that has corrupted democratic control over the essential question of war or peace.

This military-industrial-congressional complex requires that the expensive weapon systems be used from time to time. Otherwise, the public might wake up and ask why tax-payers' money is spent on weapons instead of schools, hospitals, health care or bridges that don't fall down. Weapons need to be tested in real life situations, used up (to make way for more), and demonstrated for sale to client states. But one cannot openly fire weapons at other countries for such reasons. Thus the Complex creates the need for ideological justification of war. For over forty years, the "communist threat" did the trick. The Complex was briefly in a state of shock when Gorbachev spoiled everything by abruptly ending the Cold War. What to do without it? The famous "think tanks", financed by private industry and servicing the MIC, went to work to devise new "threats." They found terrorism and human rights violations and Islamic extremism. Now they are trying to revive the "Russian threat".

There are many ways for a nation like the United States to advance economic interests, and there are many important interests that could profit just as well from a less bellicose line of action. The grip of the Complex on policy-making dictates choices that are sometimes quite irrational. Diplomacy and negotiations have become dying arts, because threats of military action are the easy reflexes. There are people capable of such practices, but they are marginalized. The military-industrial-congressional complex has its own institutional inertia that escapes from any clear conscious control.

Within this self-perpetuating mechanism, groups and individual strategists emerge with ideas of how to use the Complex. One of the most influential is Zbigniew Brzezinski, whose father was a Polish ambassador to Canada. Brzezinski has spelled out his strategic thinking in a significant book, *The Great Chessboard*. He gives priority to isolating Russia from Western Europe in order to prevent a harmonious unification of the Eurasian landmass which would mean the end of United States hegemony.

Brzezinski is sometimes in conflict with the powerful pro-Israel lobby. Their priorities sometimes conflict. Then there is the Cuban lobby, whose virulence is waning with generation change. In regard to Yugoslavia, there was an influential Croatian lobby, and there still is a well-endowed Albanian lobby. Various lobbies, sometimes claiming to represent some ethnic group in the United States, influence US policy in ways that may be quite contrary to what one could reasonably consider American national interest. Their success comes from the fact that their aims may fill the vital need of the military-industrial complex to find enemies and proclaim crusades – for democracy, for human rights, against evil dictators, against terrorism, and so on. These crusades provide justification for the United States' endless arms buildup.

### Yugoslavia as experimental terrain

The ideals proclaimed are often violated by the actions undertaken in their name. The treatment of the Serbs by the "International Community" in the name of "human rights" has been a constant violation of human rights. It is not just that their country has been bombed and torn to pieces – a process that may not be finished. Worse than that, they have been treated as pariahs by the powers that bombed and dispossessed them, and blamed by a shameful NATO-sponsored Tribunal at The Hague for all that has been done to them.

The Serbs have been used for over fifteen years as guinea pigs in a Great Power experiment. The experiment has many sides.

First of all, the Serbs have been the guinea pigs in an experiment in propaganda demonization. This has been a more or less spontaneous experiment, which various actors: the German media, to start with, followed rapidly by the U.S. public relations firm Ruder-Finn, working hand in hand with the breakaway Croatian government of Franjo Tudjman, the very active Croatian lobby in the United States and Canada, the Islamic party of Alija Izetbegovic, the Albanian lobby in the United States, and a number of American politicians, such as former Senator Bob Dole and the late Congressman Tom Lantos. The propaganda techniques used against the Serbs can be used against any country that the United States selects as a target.

They have been guinea pigs in the use of weapons using depleted uranium.

They have been guinea pigs in bringing a defenseless government to its knees by aerial bombing. Since the overwhelming majority of countries in the world are defenseless against US bombing, this could happen to almost anyone.

They have been guinea pigs in an experiment in political subversion, spearheaded by the notorious *Otpor*, financed and trained by the US government first to interfere with the electoral process in Yugoslavia so as to stage a "revolution" to overthrow Slobodan Milosevic. Otpor has gone on to serve its US masters in spreading similar phony revolutions in Georgia and Ukraine.

They have been guinea pigs in a scandalous judicial experiment in The Hague.

They are still guinea pigs in a disgraceful exercise of blackmail and enticement – the carrot and the stick – pursued by the European Union, which for the past decade has held out the mirage of membership in the European Union to bully Serbian leaders into more and more concessions... for which they get a few crumbs now and then, but never anything resembling recognition of Serbia's right to justice, or even to existence.

The Albanians were also used as guinea pigs. But in laboratory experiments, some rats are starved and others are fattened. The Albanian laboratory rats were fattened. This was certainly not for their own good.

The Albanians of Kosovo were used as pawns, to achieve three aims:

1. To further weaken and break up Yugoslavia, which had been the only independent socialist country in Europe which had close ties with the Third World, notably Arab countries, through the Non-Aligned Movement. Both Yugoslav socialism and non-alignment were weak and fading. But the United States wanted to wipe out all traces of such independent tendencies, just in case, as well as to weaken Serbia, considered a potential ally of Russia.

2. To provide a new "humanitarian" mission for NATO, as a pretext to change the nature of the alliance from defense of its members to "out of area" operations anywhere in the world where the United States chooses to intervene.

3. To build Camp Bondsteel, as a part of extension of US bases eastward toward both Russia and the Middle East.

For those who were willing to understand, this was obvious at the time. Since then, the real meaning of that "Fools' Crusade" has become clearer.

Kosovo is a shambles. The human results of the "crusade" are disastrous: hundreds of thousands of non-Albanians ethnically cleansed, Serbian Orthodox churches and monasteries burned and vandalized. Worst of all, ethnic hatred has been raised to the boiling point. This is the real key to "divide and rule." Even the Serbs in Kosovo will beg their NATO tormenters to remain in order to protect them from the Albanians, who have been given license to terrorize Serbs and other non-Albanians in Kosovo.

What can the Serbs do to overcome their pariah status? A quick answer in one word is, nothing.

The truth is cruel. There is nothing the Serbs can do, because the Great Powers have decided they need a pariah in that region, to keep the others in line, and the Serbs have been chosen. There is nothing the Serbs can do – but Americans and Europeans could do something. They would have to wake up first out of a deep political coma.

In May, 2000, a conservative and uniquely honest member of the German Bundestag, Willy Wimmer, attended a high-level conference in the Slovak capital Bratislava on NATO expansion and the Balkans. He was there in his capacity as Vice-President of the Parliamentary Assembly of the OSCE, along with senior military officials and prime ministers. The conference was organized by the US State Department and a think tank, the American Enterprise Institute, a well known haunt of neoconservative intellectual war strategists. In a letter to Gerhard Schröder, the German Chancellor at the time, Wimmer enumerated the conclusions of the Bratislava conference, including these crucial points:

- The war against the Federal Republic of Yugoslavia was waged in order to rectify General Eisenhower's erroneous decision, during World War II, not to station US troops in Yugoslavia. For strategic reasons, American troops must be stationed there, to make up for the missed opportunity from 1945. In short, the war was waged to build Camp Bondsteel.

- The Kosovo war represented a precedent, to be followed in the future.

- Serbia (probably for the purposes of securing an unhindered US military presence) must be permanently excluded from European development.

- NATO must gain total control over St. Petersburg's access to the Baltic Sea.

- In all processes, peoples' rights to self-determination should be favored over all other provisions or rules of international law.

The "right to self-determination" means in practice is that minorities are to be used to break up existing states. The prevailing ideology of globalization, eagerly accepted by much of the Western left, is that "rights" are above all "minority rights." Majorities are by implication oppressive. This undermines the legitimacy of nation-states from below, as economic globalization and the European Union undermine them from above. The sought-after result is the free play of economic powers, backed by military force, with very little left of democratic control in between.

Wimmer added his general observation: "It seems that the American side, for the sake of its own goals, is willing and ready to undermine, on a global scale, the international legal order, which came about as a result of the two world wars in the previous century. Force is to stand above law. Wherever international law stands in the way, it is to be removed."

To justify Serbia's "permanent exclusion from European development" the European Union keeps setting ever more stringent conditions for its eventual acceptance of Serbia. First Belgrade must violate its own constitution and deliver Milosevic to The Hague. Was that enough? No, the entire wartime leadership of Serbia, the officials and officers who tried to defend their country from the two-pronged attack of NATO bombers in the air and US-backed Albanian separatist guerillas on the ground, must be shipped to The Hague and prosecuted for constituting a "joint criminal enterprise." The world must take note: defending one's country from NATO will be considered a "joint criminal enterprise." That was not enough. Karadzic was arrested and sent to The Hague, but that is not enough. Even if enough Serbs are sent to The Hague to satisfy the Dutch government, the demand will change to recognition of independent Kosovo. There will always be a new post, a little higher than the previous one.

Milosevic was denounced as a dictator (although he was democratically elected several times) and an "extreme nationalist." So the US backed his replacement by the very legalistic Vojislav Kostunica. Before long, Kostunica turned out to be another "extreme nationalist." So he was replaced by Boris Tadic. But William Walker, the US agent who more or less invented the "Racak massacre" used as a pretext for the 1999 Kosovo war, says that Tadic is just as bad as the rest.[2] Tadic, says Walker, is "neither moderate nor reasonable" and furthermore, "each successive regime" in Belgrade has "continued with the same inflammatory nationalistic claims made by Milosevic to justify a policy of repression, of ethnic cleansing, of systemic rape, pillage and murder, not seen in Europe since the worse days of World War II."

Meanwhile, in Bosnia, the US at first imposed the moderate Milorad Dodik to replace the extreme nationalist leaders of Republika Srpska. But now Dodik is being demonized in turn. How is this done? First Haris Silajdzic, a public relations-trained, English speaking Islamist left-over from Izetbegovic's regime, used his turn in the revolving

---

2  William Walker, "A separate take from Serbia", *The Washington Times*, February 24, 2009.

Bosnian presidency last year to demand that Bosnia be centralized, abolishing Republika Srpska. In short, Silajdzic has demanded an end to the federal system established by the 1995 Dayton accords that brought an end to the war in Bosnia. Silajdzic's demand would mean in fact giving power in all of Bosnia to the majority group, the Muslims.

In response, Dodik said that in that case, Republika Srpska could hold a referendum on independence. After all, if Kosovo was allowed to secede from Serbia, why can't Republika Srpska secede from Bosnia? Because it's Serb, that's why. The cry has gone up in the media: the Serbs are causing trouble again, war may resume. Srecko Latal, a "Bosnia specialist" at the Balkan Investigative Reporting Network (BIRN) in Sarajevo, warned in February 2009 that if the Serb Republic declared independence, Croatia would send in its troops to intervene. Croatia is a member of NATO – not only de facto, as when US-backed Croatian forces drove the Serb population out of the Krajina in 1995, but de iure.

James Lyons has accused Republika Srpska's prime minister, Milorad Dodik of "emulating Montenegro's gradual path to independence" – a path that was, by the way, strewn with roses by the "International Community."[3] In Italy, Montenegro's leader Milo Djukanovic is particularly well known for, shall we say, his encouragement of low-cost cigarette smoking. Certainly Milorad Dodik is as honest a leader as the NATO-favored Djukanovic. But, says James Lyons – who has long meddled in Balkan affairs via the International Crisis Group – "Republika Srpska isn't Montenegro, and the breakup of Bosnia would be violent and probably result in the destruction of Republika Srpska."

There is no reason to believe that NATO's war against the Serbs is over.

## The Russian parallel

Yugoslavia was used as an experiment in using minorities in a multi-ethnic country to break it into small dependent client states. It seems that the main place where the lessons from this laboratory could be applied is Russia. This was no doubt in the minds of some of the strategists who steered the US military juggernaut in the direction of Yugoslavia. For some, Yugoslavia was a miniature Soviet Union.

One of these was apparently Zbigniew Brzezinski. He is still fighting with Russia over which country will dominate the lands between Poland and Russia, in particular the Ukraine, which has alternately been part of the Russian and Polish empires. Many people in the West have forgotten that Poland was once a vast empire, and most

---

3 James Lyons, "Halting the downward spiral." *The New York Times*, February 24, 2009.

Americans surely have no idea that such a thing every happened. Thus Brzezinski speaks repeatedly of "the Russian threat" to Ukraine, while the United States builds military bases all around Russia and demands that Ukraine join NATO. Nobody speaks of "the Polish threat," because only the Poles (and other people in the region) seem to remember Polish dominance of the Ukraine.

A significant parallel exists with the Balkans. The wars of Yugoslav disintegration broke out most violently in a region called the Krajina, which means borderland. So does Ukraine; it is a variant of the same Slavic root. Both Krajina and Ukraine are borderlands between Catholic Christians in the West and Orthodox Christians in the East. The population is divided between those in the East who want to retain links to Russia, and those in the West who are drawn toward Catholic lands. But in Ukraine as a whole, some seventy percent of the population is against joining NATO. Yet the US and its satellites keep speaking of Ukraine's "right" to join NATO. Nobody's right not to join NATO is ever mentioned.

The condition for Ukraine to join NATO is expelling foreign military bases from its territory. That would mean expelling Russia from its historic naval base at Sebastopol, essential for Russia's Black Sea fleet. Sebastopol is on the Crimean peninsula, inhabited by patriotic Russians, which was only made an administrative part of Ukraine by Nikita Khrushchev, a Ukrainian. Rather the way Tito, a Croat, gave almost the whole Adriatic coastline of Yugoslavia to Croatia, and generally enforced administrative borders detrimental to the Serbs.

As the same causes may have the same effects, the US insistence on "liberating" Ukraine from Russian influence may have the same effect as the West's insistence on "liberating" the Catholic Croats from the Orthodox Serbs. That effect is war. But instead of a small war against the Serbs, who had neither the means nor even the will to fight the West (since they largely thought they were part of it), a war in Ukraine would mean a war with Russia. A nuclear superpower, and one that will not stand idly by while the United States continues to move its fleet and its air bases to the edges of Russian territory, both in the Black Sea and in the Baltic, on land, sea and air.

Every day, the United States is busy expanding NATO, training forces, building bases, making deals. This goes on constantly but is scarcely reported by the media. The citizens of NATO countries have no idea what they are being led into.

U.S. President Barack Obama looks like an improvement over the last one, but he is surrounded by the same people who waged the 1999 war: Joe Biden, a ferocious anti-Serb as Vice President, and Hillary Clinton, who is said to have urged her reluctant husband to bomb the Serbs, as secretary of state. The United States is technically bankrupt, but the imaginary money keeps pouring into the weapons industry. Obama is not a dictator. The United States is a complex machine, not a one-man dictatorship. The military-industrial-congressional complex is on automatic pilot. Presidents come and presidents go, but the Complex follows its own momentum. The new president is following the momentum into an endless war in Afghanistan. Without pressure from citizens for real change, and not merely inspirational rhetoric, even the best-intentioned president will be swept along by the Complex.

War was easy when it meant the destruction of a helpless and harmless Serbia, with no casualties among the NATO aggressors. But war with Russia – a fierce super-power with a nuclear arsenal – will not be so much fun. If no one cares about history, justice or the plight of people whose country has been torn apart, perhaps concern for mere survival may wake people up to what is going on. That is something we can try to do.

As for the Serbs – the only thing they can do is what they have done so far: hang onto their famous sense of graveyard humor, and keep in mind that there is more to the world than NATO and the "International Community." This, too, will pass.

# Kosovo: To What End?

*Gregory R. Copley*[1]

Ten years have elapsed since the US-led aerial bombardment by forces of a number of North Atlantic Treaty Organization (NATO) states of Serbia. They acted on the pretext — subsequently found to have been massively flawed by deliberately contrived or faulty "intelligence" — of stopping the "persecution," even "genocide", of the ethnic Albanian population of the Serbian province of Kosovo.

Kosovo is a name which, to most of the world, has come and gone. It is recalled as a few anguished moments of television coverage, neither understood nor even explained. The dust, it appears, has settled on this part of the Balkans; the turbulence, as far as a disinterested world is concerned, has subsided; the substance of the dispute forgotten before it was even known.

-Yet the affair leading up to Kosovo's unilateral declaration of independence (UDI) from Serbia on February 17, 2008, is not over. It set in train a series of events which transformed the entire Black Sea/Caspian Sea energy basin and its network of energy supply from the Caucasus and Central Asia to Europe. We have yet to see the final outcome. It was an affair which, from its earliest gestation as an overt secessionist movement in the beginning of the 1990s, highlighted inept and corrupt policy management, in Serbia, the European Union, the United States, and the United Nations. It was as if no one could understand the ramifications of their actions.

The outcome of those actions was not unforeseeable, however. This writer and his team at the International Strategic Studies Association (ISSA), forecast it to the

---

1 Gregory Copley is President of the International Strategic Studies Association (ISSA), Editor-in-Chief of *Defense & Foreign Affairs* publications, and the Director of Intelligence at the Global Information System (GIS), an on-line global intelligence service.

rump Yugoslav Government and the Serbian leadership as early as 1992. We warned senior officials in Belgrade that the Serbian province of Kosovo and Metohija, the southwestern Serbian region of Raška (Sandzak), and the Preševo Valley would soon become centers of agitation for independence, and that the US would back such claims. Our claims were met in Belgrade with incredulity. We were told that the information we conveyed could not possibly be true: these were internal Serbian areas; there was only (at that time) a smattering of anti-government hostility by those Muslims and Albanians who had supported the Bosnian and Croatian moves for independence from Yugoslavia. In any event, why would the US Government do this? Had Serbia not always been an ally of the US, notably proving its loyalty in World War II?

The die, however, had been cast. The incoming US Clinton Administration of 1993 to 2001 — or, rather, President William Clinton personally — had already thrown in its lot with the Albanian lobby in the US. Even in his days as Governor of Arkansas, Clinton had been shown to have made questionable deals with the Albanians, a pattern which persisted for many years. Moreover, even as Governor Clinton was preparing his race for the US Presidency, the Albanian and Bosnian lobbies in the US and Europe had, with the help of billions of dollars of funds gained from narco-trafficking and other crimes, made the case in the Western media: "Serbs bad, Muslims good".

The pattern of US support for the Kosovo Albanian separatists was not about to be changed. On the contrary, it received enormous support from other quarters, including private financiers such as George Soros, who stood to benefit financial from the independence of Kosovo from Serbia. It is noteworthy that the current US Secretary of State is the wife and partner of former President Clinton. The pattern of US support for Kosovo, and against the Serbs of Kosovo and the remaining rump of Serbia are most unlikely to change.

The ISSA had then, and has now, no stake in the outcome of affairs in the Balkans. Even-handed intelligence-gathering or analysis was not in demand, however; the pressure was to conform to the mainstream media view, which was to become the mainstream political view in the West. Our forecasting proved accurate. Kosovo was to be forcibly ripped from Serbia, although not with the global acquiescence which Washington had believed possible. The campaigns simmering outside Kosovo and Metohija, in Raška and the Preševo Valley, would move to the front burner.

The Kosovo UDI set a precedent which would come back to haunt the United States and the European Union, particularly when the Russian Federation backed the resistance by South Ossetia to the military invasion by a US-backed Government of Georgia in August 2008. Russia immediately recognized the declaration of sovereignty

of South Ossetia and Abkhazia, citing the precedent of Kosovo's US-backed UDI –
even though, in fact, South Ossetia and Abkhazia had never been integrated into Georgia, whereas Kosovo had been an integral component of Serbia. The Kosovo precedent
which saw the collapse of the Georgian initiative to seize South Ossetia and Abkhazia
was more than mere tit-for-tat: it has totally transformed the pattern of energy trading
which supports the viability of the European Union.

The failure of Georgia to prevail carried with it the failure of US influence in
the Eastern Black Sea region. The first casualty was US influence in Azerbaijan, the key
hub on the Western shores of the Caspian Sea for oil and gas — including transshipped
oil and gas from Central Asia — through Georgia to the Black Sea and on to Western
Europe. The government of Azerbaijan, which had relied on Western support to assist
its long-sought freedom from Moscow's control, was now shown to be in a vulnerable
position. The US had failed to extend its writ east of the Black Sea, and Azerbaijan had
to accommodate the Russian Federation.

Immediately after the collapse of the Georgian military misadventure and after
a short, poorly prepared visit to Baku by US Vice-President Richard Cheney, Azerbaijan's President Ilham Aliyev felt compelled to fly to Moscow and come to terms with
Russia's reaffirmed regional authority. Azerbaijan would henceforth ship some of its
energy through Russian pipelines and routes, limiting the independence which Caspian and Central Asian energy producers had hoped to achieve. The Georgian collapse
at the same time ended some of the growing centrality which Turkey was gaining in the
Caspian/Black Sea basins' energy hub. And Western Europe's dependence on Russia
for energy became more complete.

This is the key geopolitical outcome of the US support for Kosovo's independence, quite apart from the longer-term precedent it set for national sub-units in other
countries. Those who took heart from the Kosovo secession included, among others,
the Turkish government in its quest to wrench Northern Cyprus from the Republic
of Cyprus; the Armenians who wished to seize control of Nagorno-Karabakh from
Azerbaijan; the Algerians who wished to take Moroccan Sahara from the Kingdom of
Morocco; and so on. Ultimately, it also supported the cause of the creation of a new
Kurdish state out of Iraq, Turkey, Iran, and part of Syria. It gave encouragement to the
cause of Quebec's separation from Canada. The list goes on.

The US State Department, locked into support for the Albanians, has said that
the case of Kosovo's independence was *sui generis*: unique unto itself, and not a precedent for any others. The reality, of course, was that the Kosovo affair was *sui generis*

only in the minds of State Department officials. One must wonder at what they were thinking, drinking, or smoking, to make such a claim without blushing.

There have been a number of cases of the birth of nations in the post-Cold War period: Timor Leste, Eritrea, Kosovo, Montenegro, and so on, without counting the re-assertion of independence of former federal units such as Croatia or Slovenia. The question is how these fit within the original UN framework and the later (often mutually contradictory) Helsinki Accords, which talk first about the sanctity of sovereign borders and then about the rights of peoples to self-determination.

The reality is that the rigid structures proposed by the creation of the United Nations in 1945 were to freeze the global *status quo* achieved by the victorious powers of World War II. The UN failed to adapt, however. The constant societal evolution which had moved to post-Westphalian forms of sovereignty in the 20th century was supposed to remain frozen. The UN Charter somehow hypothesized that mankind had achieved the ultimate definition of nationhood and global governance, and would adapt no more.

The process failed to account for the growth of the global population (from 2.5 billion in 1950 to almost 7 billion today); that the Cold War, which had its roots in World War II, would end and lead the world from bipolarism back to multipolarism; and that technology, globalization, and growing wealth would transform social patterns, expectations, and needs. The world, nonetheless, clings to concepts and institutions it knows or believes in. Even Rome crumbled and collapsed, yet we failed to learn how to manage great change. Had we learned we would have moved from success to success; instead, as with the collapse of Rome, we face a return to some new form of Dark Age, in which economic collapse attends political confusion and malaise. With that come a decline in investment, a decline in education and healthcare, and a decline in life expectancy and in the quality of life.

Kosovo was an example of the indulgence of a superpower, the United States, because of massive corruption by a number of politicians in the US and in the United Nations structure. ISSA highlighted and documented how, for example, the key UN official involved in "managing" the Kosovo issue was bribed by Kosovo Albanians. German intelligence officials monitored the case, amassing significant evidence of the financial corruption of the official, former Finnish President Martti Ahtisaari. The evidence was shown to other NATO member governments. The UN's own office for investigations refused to follow up the evidence against their own official, who was later to be awarded the Nobel Peace Prize.

This does not even touch on the issue of the internal criminality of the group of Albanians who seized a section of someone else's land and turned it into a "country" with some degree of international recognition. ISSA documented, time and again, the extent of involvement by Kosovo Albanians — linked to the supposedly defunct KLA — in a wide range of criminal and terrorist activity which has greatly undermined Western Europe, and now, increasingly, Eastern Europe.

The KLA, or by whatever name it or its sub-groups now choose to be called, have been at the forefront of narco-trafficking, white slaving, and weapons trafficking in Western Europe and, increasingly, in North America. Given the US and British governments' support for the KLA, it is difficult to get official acknowledgement of the fact that it is at the heart of much of the violent crime in Europe today as well as in the US, let alone to get acknowledgement of the fact that the KLA provided, or facilitated the provision of much of the explosives, training, and *matériel* used by Islamist terrorists in Spain, Britain, Morocco, and elsewhere. European and other governments do acknowledge that the "Albanian mafia" has grown to dominate organized crime, without questioning where it gets its safe-havens, its narcotics, or its human flesh for trafficking.

The work of ISSA's investigators in the Balkans has resulted in massive files of data, much of which formed the basis of intelligence estimates for a number of governments that subscribe to its Global Information System (GIS) or its unclassified journals, such as *Defense & Foreign Affairs* publications. Friends and contacts died in the collection of the data, and yet it is difficult to name a politician or a newspaper editor who would, when faced with incontrovertible evidence, change his mind and refute the superficial or inaccurate reporting on the Balkans. Others, complicit in the transformation of values which the Kosovo case represented (along with the companion usurpation of justice in Bosnia-Herzegovina and elsewhere in the Balkans), merely shrug their shoulders: what can we do?

I will not recite all of the evidence we brought to deaf ears and blind eyes through the 1990s and beyond. Neither will I cite all the instances in which my colleagues and I witnessed the smugness and corruption inside Serbia and outside it which caused the collapse of values and integrity of NATO, and the end of the moral supremacy of the West. That does not imply that those who opposed the West, or NATO, gained in moral stature in this whole affair. They did not, but they profited greatly by the decline of the West's supposed commitment to high values, and to its allies.

We have all been demeaned by the corruption which has touched our systems. We have been brought into contact, and – indeed – into partnership, with the callous depravity of those who traffic in narcotics, human beings, and the corruption of hierarchies which have taken centuries to build. We have allowed this because we would not read history and because we valued immediate gratification beyond wisdom.

We have all become aged and tired by this hypocrisy, to the point where we have lost the moral authority to demand that the youth of today learn from history and build upon the structures we had been handed by our own ancestors.

With Kosovo, the modern world, East and West, abandoned virtue.

# Imperial Democracy and Global Jihad

## Gregory M. Davis[1]

T he breakup of Yugoslavia and the de facto secession of Kosovo-Metohija from Serbia mark a significant episode in the post-Cold War struggle between three major world-historical forces: US-led globalization, jihad, and the old nation-state system. These three forces are the current expressions of the three civilizations that have competed for pre-eminence in the Balkan Peninsula for a thousand years: the West, Islam, and the Orthodox East.

In somewhat simplistic but meaningful terms, the Orthodox East has once again found itself squeezed in a vice between two imperialistic, violent ideologies, happy to wreck Balkan civilization for their own misguided self-interest. Despite its Christian elements, the West has once again shown itself willing to undermine the Christian East even while strengthening Islam, the ancient enemy of both. To that end, during the Yugoslav civil wars of the 1990s, the US-led West encouraged the violent, as opposed to pacific, breakup of Yugoslavia; supported a hard-core Islamic supremacist, Alija Izetbegovic, in his efforts to build the first Islamic state in Europe; and supported both diplomatically and militarily Muslim militants in Bosnia and Kosovo in their efforts to kill and ethnically cleanse Serb civilians.

---

1 Dr. Gregory M. Davis, an occasional contributor to *Human Events, WorldNet Daily* and Chronicles, is author of *Religion of Peace?* and producer and director of the feature documentary *Islam: What the West Needs to Know.*

To some extent, the Western-backed assault on Yugoslavia may be regarded as exploitation of a target of opportunity. By 1991, Communism had fallen apart all over Europe. One of the Yugoslav republics, Croatia, was an old ally of a newly-reunified, resurgent Germany, who was happy to bring her old confederate into the Western fold. Yugoslavia itself had endeavored to cauterize its internal ethnic and religious fault lines with only incomplete success.

The West's villainization of the Serbs was easy. First, the Serbs posed no conceivable threat to Western interests, so there was no danger in antagonizing them; second, they showed themselves unable to present their side of the story to Western audiences with any efficacy. Villainizing them, therefore, was basically costless. It is far easier to pick on a weak, largely innocent party than a strong, culpable one with the capacity to retaliate. By throwing the Serbs under the bus, one of the West's objectives was to court Islamic world opinion. Commenting on US support for the secession of Kosovo from Serbia, the late Tom Lantos, Chairman of the US House of Representatives Foreign Affairs Committee, put it this way:

> *Just a reminder to the predominantly Muslim-led government[s] in this world that here is yet another example that the United States leads the way for the creation of a predominantly Muslim country in the very heart of Europe. This should be noted by both responsible leaders of Islamic governments, such as Indonesia, and also for jihadists of all color and hue. The United States' principles are universal, and in this instance, the United States stands foursquare for the creation of an overwhelmingly Muslim country in the very heart of Europe.*

In short, the West has been trying to appease the Islamic world by supporting their cause in the Balkans in the hope of benefiting from, one supposes, more freely available oil and fewer aircraft crashed into crowded office buildings. The West's continued persecution of Serbia, however, years after Yugoslavia's demise, indicates deeper forces at work. America's support of Muslim Albanian terrorists in Kosovo, in particular, bears noting.

It is clear that, beyond even horribly distorted considerations of realpolitik, there is an ideological affinity between the contemporary West and Islam that has escaped most observers. This affinity has enabled the West and Islam to work hand in glove against a common enemy, namely, the old nation-state system and its leading representatives in the Orthodox Christian, Slavic East. Understanding this affinity is key to understanding Western motives in the Balkans and the continued anti-Russian, anti-Slavic, anti-Orthodox attitude prevalent in the West, especially the United States.

At first blush, the claim that the West and Islam would be able to cooperate in any significant way appears insupportable. The West and Islam seem to be polar opposites. Islam, in its traditional form, mandates the imposition of Sharia law over the globe, which includes such niceties as stoning for adultery, amputation of limbs for theft, a blanket moratorium on the construction of Jewish and Christian houses of worship and all evangelism, the forcible conversion of pagans and atheists on pain of death, the proscription of usury, and the execution of apostates – to start with. While Islam seeks the political supremacy of "god" and his law, the West today seems intent on shoving God and His laws as far out of the public square as possible. Western man is now sovereign; he can do no wrong. Needless to say, he wouldn't last long under Sharia.

Yet while there are major differences between Islam and the West, there are powerful similarities. Islam from its beginnings aspired to global mastery. According to Muhammad and the Koran, the law of Allah is prescribed for the globe; any nation or individual who does not submit to Islamic rule is ipso facto in a state of rebellion with Allah and must be brought into obedience by force. Islam, in short, constituted an early form of globalization. Islam does not recognize the legitimacy of nations, peoples, or governments except insofar as they submit to Islamic overlordship.

So it is with the West today. Only if a nation-state is willing to play ball with the West on its terms is it considered legitimate. Like Islam, the West's ambitions are global: there is no longer any long-term accommodation possible between the West and alternative systems. The West employs its parochial definitions of "human rights," "democracy," "free markets," etc. to cajole and browbeat nations that refuse to submit to its economic and strategic hegemony, or it employs economic pressure and, if that fails, military force. Nations such as Pakistan, Kazakhstan, and Saudi Arabia, whose record on "human rights" etc. is checkered at best, escape serious Western pressure thanks to their willingness to play the West's political and economic ballgame.

The common ground then between the West and Islam is that they are both programs of globalization that have as their object the destruction of the old nation-state system based on the sovereignty of states and nationhood defined by ethnic, linguistic, cultural, and territorial commonalities. Both Islam and the contemporary West are essentially empires that seek global hegemony and do not recognize the legitimacy of alternative forms of political, social, and cultural organization if they refuse to submit to the suzerainty of the larger system.

With this in mind, it is not hard to see how the West and Islam would connive in the destruction of independent nation-states such as Yugoslavia and Serbia have that historically resisted both systems. Following the breakup of Soviet communism, the Eastern European countries, especially the Orthodox ones, became the leading champions of the old nation-state system. Thanks to the Iron Curtain, these countries were relatively preserved from the poisonous effects of Western consumerism, multicultural-ism, and general social-cultural suicide. Since the fall of Soviet Communism, most of the former east-bloc states have been falling over themselves to jump on the Western bandwagon. Those former Communist states such as Russia and Serbia that retained more of their Slavic, Orthodox, and national consciousness, and which consequently present the greatest potential resistance to Western and Islamic expansion, attract the antipathy of both.

We should bear in mind that Western policies for the past thirty years have been substantially pro-Islam and pro-jihadist: US support for the mujahedeen fighting the Soviets in Afghanistan; EC and later EU encouragement of Muslim immigration into Europe and the propagation of Islamic identity among Europe's Muslims; the re-placement by Western force of the relatively secular regime of Saddam Hussein with a government based in Sharia; criticism of Russia for effective counter-jihad measures in Chechnya and the Caucuses; support for elections in the Palestinian territories with the resulting success of the jihadist group Hamas; etc. Furthermore, it is easily demon-strated that, for all the bluster about fighting the "war on terror," the US is not really that serious about reducing the threat of Islamic terrorism.

In such a context, Western economic, political, and military support for Alija Izetbegovic's Islamic regime in Bosnia and the Muslim terrorist group, KLA, in Ko-sovo, seems almost unsurprising. Former Vice President Richard Cheney remarked shortly after leaving office that another major terrorist attack is not a question of *if* but *when*. Yet reducing the likelihood of another such attack would be hugely aided by a few simple steps that the US and the West refuse to adopt. Years following Septem-ber 11, the most spectacular national-security-intelligence failure in world history, the United States, the most awesome economic and military power of all time, has yet to gain control of its borders or to name the enemy that it is supposedly fighting. Rather, it insists on largely uncontrolled borders and in affirming, time and again, the prepos-terous notion that Islam is "a religion of peace" in contradiction to the religion's own core texts.

The failure to implement serious border-control measures or to name the enemy indicates that the US is less interested in protecting itself from terrorist attack than it is in advancing the cause of its own global empire, what might be called imperial democracy. The uncomfortable reality is that the building of the empire is significantly aided by the persistence of a grassroots, violent, religious ideology such as Islam. By abetting the growth of Islamic fundamentalism both in the Islamic world and in the West, the Western empire both undermines old national identities and fosters a justification for its own ever-expanding power. Islam is a perfect foil for Western imperialism: it provides a powerful solvent to the old nation-states that compliments the cultural alienation that is the West's weapon of choice. Furthermore, Islam's global pretensions help justify the Western overseas military and intelligence adventures (e.g. the "global war on terror").

While the ideologies of Islam and the contemporary West both aspire to global mastery, the fact is that the latter is increasingly the only game in town. While small groups of Orthodox Muslims continue to press their violent, jihadist agenda sporadically around the globe – with the occasional spectacular success – Western economic, cultural, and military power is, for the most part, carrying everything before it. The Islamic states themselves, with only a few exceptions, are integrating themselves into the Western-dominated global game. Islam, while still possessed of an abiding religious orientation, remains fragmented and largely incapable of bringing new nations into the Islamic fold save for the tactic of populating them with Muslims (and this only insofar as other nations permit them, e.g. Western Europe). Increasingly, Islam appears to be emptying from the center. Islamic governments tread a fine line between the mandates of Sharia, which are fundamentally impractical, and the overwhelming military and economic power of the West. More and more, Islamic states are showing themselves willing to play ball with the West while pushing strict Sharia and jihad to the periphery, e.g. the Muslim diaspora in Europe. Syria, Jordan, Egypt, Saudi Arabia, Iraq, Indonesia, Kazakhstan, Turkey, and most Islamic countries are integrated into the Western-dominated economic and military global order even while significant elements in those countries wax nostalgic for the good old days when Islam was the terror of the globe. The distinctly Islamic policies of those states, such as they are, come mainly in the form of enforcing as much Sharia at home as needed to pacify Muslim conservatives and subsidizing jihadist terrorism abroad. Their leaders are happy to shake hands with the leading infidel powers because they know those powers hold the economic and military trump cards.

These trump cards are played with remarkable consistency almost regardless of the partisan orientation of particular Western governments. Whatever the differences between the major poles of "mainstream" political thought in the West today, advancing the cause of imperial democracy is a point of general agreement, especially in the US. Under a right-wing US administration, imperialism assumes an "America-first" veneer; under a left-wing administration, "multilateralism," "co-operation," and "engagement" serve as its justifications. Clinton's Yugoslav adventures were generally portrayed as "humanitarian" actions; the Asian wars of the two Bushes were painted as "patriotic" wars to safeguard US interests and get the bad guys. Grains of truth in all cases, of course, atop heaps of falsehood. US-led Western imperialism thus takes on different shades depending on the partisan flavor of the sitting administration, but the overall program advances largely unhindered.

Neither the left nor the right can provide effective resistance to the general imperial program. On the left, we have the running criticism of US-led foreign and defense policy as provocative, destructive, and unjust. There is much truth there. Unhappily, bound up with such criticism is a standing apology for everybody else, including the Islamic world, as innocent victims of US aggression, and contempt for the remaining noble elements of the West such as Christianity and genuine patriotism. On the right, there is recognition (more so) of the dangers and distortions of non-Western ideologies, such as Islam, and of the progressive cultural suicide of the West, yet there is little understanding of the failures of American policy or of the destructiveness of Western military adventurism. The errors of the one are pounced on by the other, and vice versa, such that the inane left-right ping pong match proceeds unimpeded.

The actual policies of both wings, however, prove remarkably similar. Each of the US administrations since the end of the Cold War has engaged, at one time or another, in a major overseas adventure that directly involved US combat forces. The continuity goes back even further, but with the decline of Soviet Communism, there is no major counterweight to American-led power, and the imperial tendencies of the West have burst into the open. Gulf War I, the NATO campaign against the Bosnian Serbs, the NATO campaign against Serbia, Afghanistan, Gulf War II, and now the Obama administration's new Afghan offensive are really aspects of the same program even while Republican and Democratic administrations find somewhat different ways of justifying them. Obama's supporters thirsting for "change" have in fact got pledges to keep 50,000 troops in Iraq indefinitely and the prospect of a much bigger war in Afghanistan. Imperial democracy marches on.

With Serbia effectively inoculated (at least for the time being), the West has retrained its sites. The fate of Yugoslavia and of Serbia is one that the Western empire would very much like to extend to the current champion of the nation-state system and historic ally of the Serbs, Russia. What distinguishes Russia from other countries today is a) she is a nation-state – a territorial, ethnic, linguistic, religious whole – and

b) she has demonstrated both a will and a capacity to remain that way. Like Serbia, her national-religious consciousness runs deeper than most Westerners can fathom. Following the disastrous 1990s in which Russia adopted Western-style "reforms," Vladimir Putin led his nation back onto a path of national regeneration that has stirred the ire of the Western globalizers. One of Russia's greatest offences is the rejection of the Western "separation" of church and state.

In the Orthodox tradition, the nation is an organic whole that cannot be categorically compartmentalized into political versus religious, secular versus spiritual. To "separate" the church from the state is akin to separating the soul from the body, i.e., to kill it. The fruits of the West's "separation" are everywhere apparent: abandonment of churches, rising crime and delinquency, divorce, climbing suicide rates, and the waning of the social survival impulse in the form of collapsing birth rates. These problems are not unique to the West, but they prevail in proportion to the extent to which a given society has adopted the contemporary Western program of moral-cultural suicide.

The ongoing US-led persecution of Serbia is in line with the persistent anti-Russian attitude that is the current centerpiece of Western strategy. Since the collapse of Soviet hegemony in Europe, the US-led West has instituted a series of highly aggressive policies that evince a total disregard for Russia's traditional sphere of influence. The expansion of NATO to Russia's borders, for example, will directly involve the United States and all of Western Europe in any conflict between Russia and the Baltic countries, which Russia ruled for centuries.

For Westerners to get some idea of the extreme lengths US-led anti-Russian policy has reached since the close of the Cold War, they should try to see things from Russia's point of view. How would America react, one wonders, if the old USSR had effected policies comparable to America's since 1989? Try this: Twenty years ago, the democratic regimes of the NATO countries disintegrate and are replaced with pro-Soviet regimes that expel American troops. Next, in 1991, the United States itself suffers an internal upheaval that sees a massive economic contraction and the secession of Alaska, Hawaii, and Texas. During this time of US weakness, civil war breaks out in the United Kingdom in which the Warsaw Pact intervenes and facilitates the breakup of the country. In 1998, the US defaults on its debt and the dollar collapses. Then, in 1999, unhappy with English "oppression" of the Scots, the USSR bombs London for seventy-eight days. The Soviet Union then extends Warsaw Pact guarantees to Western Europe, Canada, and the former US states of Hawaii and Alaska. Now the USSR is talking about concluding a mutual defense agreement with Texas and building a missile shield in Quebec to safeguard against rogue Latin American states. Absurd? The foregoing is a fair approximation of how Western policy appears from Russian standpoint. That such an aggressive policy is sincerely defended in the West as reasonable and defensive testifies to the unlimited extent of Western aims.

While those aims entail the subversion and ultimate destruction of strong nation-states such as Russia, the process of national disintegration is not only for foreign consumption. The West so far has been most successful in undermining its own constituent nation-states The general strategy of the empire is to undermine the natural and organic means of political and social organization so as to leave its own power unchecked – even at the expense of its own constituent nation-states.

Imperial democracy is truly supranational. The nation-states in the West are almost as much targets for social, political, economic, and territorial dissolution as non-Western ones. The Western-sponsored ideological movements of multiculturalism and moral relativism (to name but two) serve to delegitimize the principles of common ethnicity, language, religion, and territory around which peoples and nation-states have historically organized. By leaving the official institutions outwardly intact while eviscerating them from within, the empire can implement its aims without fear of effective organized resistance from within the legal/constitutional channels of power. The money and media interests that serve the empire's agenda have become the true centers of power, the real government, even while the official legislative, executive, and judicial institutions retain the appearance of authority. The beauty of "democracy" is that it engenders a constantly shifting institutional landscape that is easily manipulated. The de-legitimation of ethnicity (in particular among the dominant Western one), language, religion (in particular, Christianity), and territory forestalls any attempt by representatives within the official institutions to reclaim their national inheritances.

The Western imperial program to wreck what is left of the nation-state system on a global scale leaves Western conservatives in a bind. During the Cold War it was still possible to regard the West, the adversary of revolutionary communism, as a conservative force in the world. With the aggressive and highly destructive extension of the Western empire in the post-Soviet period, however, this position is no longer tenable. Western conservatives are now in the position of defending the actions of the world's leading revolutionary force. True-blooded Western conservatives need to reject the assumptions that have elevated Western-style democracy to the level of a religion with a global mandate. For all the reasons that Western conservatives mistrusted Communism and should mistrust Islam, they must discard the false god of imperial democracy as well.

The "neoconservatives" that insist on pushing Western democracy on the rest of the world at the point of a gun must be rudely dismissed from conservative ranks. The discomfiting reality is that, for Western conservatives to remain conservative, they must be willing to take up the cause of the truly conservative powers left in the world, namely, those nation-states intent on resisting the Western empire and retaining their historic identity. Acknowledging the West's crimes against the Serbs, the continuing injustices of the unbalanced Hague war crimes tribunal, and the imperialistic nature of the Western occupation of Kosovo would be the right places to start. Supporting the national and religious reawakening of Russia, as a healthy model for nation-states everywhere, would be another.

The unyielding expansion of the Western empire is today the greatest threat to peace in the world. The diplomatic and military campaigns directed against the Serbs during the past eighteen years, and the West's willingness to ally itself with as alien and destructive an ideology as Islam, are some of the most vivid examples of the lengths to which the US-led West will go to impose its will on nations that seek to resist its democratic empire. The West's treatment of Serbia should be a cautionary tale for nations such as Russia, who have so far resisted Western pressure by virtue of their greater size and power.

The West now offers the nations of the world only two options: submit to Western economic and strategic dominance and remain intact, or seek to remain outside the Western orbit and face destruction. In either case, the result – the loss of independence and nationhood – is the same. It is the same sort of "choice" that revolutionary ideologies from Islam to Communism have offered and it should galvanize resistance from true conservatives everywhere. Like all revolutionary programs that have sought world mastery, imperial democracy can only culminate in material and spiritual oblivion. The Western political and economic order is already showing the strain. The question is whether genuine forces of conservation in the West can succeed in reigning in the excesses of imperial democracy before a Western internal collapse or a violent confrontation with Russia. So far, there is not much ground for optimism.

# Historical Background

Though few English and even fewer American history books tell us much about her, in the 300 years which lie between the Norman Conquest of England and the death of Edward III, Serbia was one of the strongest and most culturally and economically advanced states in the whole of Europe.

The preconditions for the creation of the Serbian nation came about in the early seventh century, when southern Slavs spread out widely across the Balkan Peninsula and formed numerous small principalities. Constantinople viewed them initially as a passing irritant, for even when various barbarian tribes ransacked the walled cities, they soon left. Slavs, on the other hand, were not nomadic types. They tended to settle and change the ethnic character of the area.

Byzantine rulers, notably Emperor Basil II, tried to drive the Slavs out, but military failure eventually gave way to political realism. There were more serious problems confronting the Empire. There were the Persians, Muslim Arabs, and Seljuk Turks, who kept the Byzantines occupied in the east for several centuries. In the west the Normans and the Venetians were sapping Byzantium's military strength. The Slavs, for their part, exploited these troubles to expand and solidify their positions. Even after Constantinople managed to restore much of its imperial prestige, it was challenged in the north by the invading Magyars, who waged four successive wars against Byzantium.

Once the beleaguered Byzantine emperors accepted Serbs and Bulgars as permanent inhabitants of the Balkans, they proceeded to co-opt them. Constantinople succeeded in baptizing the early Serbian rulers around 870 AD. Mass conversion of the Serbs to Christianity soon followed, accompanied by strong political and cultural influences from the Empire. The path to early "ethnogenesis" of the Serbs was opened up on the basis of a common Christian culture, greatly helped by the translation of biblical and liturgical texts into the Slavonic vernacular and by the alphabets adapted to the language of the Slavs.

The first Serbian ruler of international stature was Stefan Nemanja (1166-1196). Talented and determined, he took advantage of the weaknesses of the Byzantine Empire and greatly extended his authority, territorially and politically. He ruled the best part of today's Serbia (including the state's heartland of Kosovo) and Montenegro. Eventually Nemanja abdicated the throne and withdrew to a monastery, appointing his middle son, Stefan, to replace him. Nemanja joined his youngest son Sava – also a monk – at Mt. Athos. Together they built the monastery of Chilandar, which for the ensuing eight centuries was to play an important role in nurturing the Serbian spirituality and culture.

The respectful son later wrote a biography of his father, the founder of the dynasty and Serbian statehood. *The Life of Master Simeon* dealt not with the secular Nemanja but with the spiritual Simeon, the monk of noble heritage. In addition to countless church manuals, canonic and instructive texts for use by monks and priests, Sava also tried his hand at verse. Being the most traveled Serb of his time, he visited and personally knew Byzantine emperors Alexis III Angelus, Theodore I Lascaris, and John III Vatatzes, and the patriarchs of Constantinople and of Nicaea. Sava knew the frailty of men, the mighty and the weak. In a poem, entitled *Word about Torment*, he writes:

> *Dead am I even before my death,*
> *I sentence myself even before the judge does,*
> *Even before the ceaseless pain sets in.*
> *I am already tortured by my own agony.*

Nemanja's middle son *Stefan Nemanjic* (1196-1227) enjoyed the support of the Byzantine Empire and managed to maintain his father's domains. When the Crusaders led by the Venetians conquered Constantinople in 1204, Stefan turned to the West. Through clever political maneuvering he managed to remove threats from Hungary, from the Latin Empire of the Crusaders, from the revived Bulgaria, and from the newly independent rulers in the Byzantine provinces. He greatly improved Serbia's reputation and rank by receiving a royal crown from the Pope (1217), which among his descendants and heirs brought him the appellation of the "First-Crowned King" – Stefan *Prvovencani.*

The King's youngest brother, Sava, sought to create unified ecclesiastical framework within Serbia. He obtained agreement from the Byzantine Emperor and from the Patriarch to form a separate archbishopric. He was appointed Archbishop of Serbia in 1219 in Nicaea, and it was decided that his successors would be chosen and appointed by the Serbs themselves. This gave an impetus to the vibrant growth of the Serbian Church. New bishoprics were founded, with their sees in the monasteries where the priests were educated, and the books necessary for the life of the church were copied. Sava provided for a translation of the Byzantine code of church laws and rules for the use of the clergy, the *Nomokanon*.

Serbian rulers, in a manner of speaking, were seeking to pursue a "non-aligned" policy. They fought Byzantium, but could never rid themselves of its spell. Serbia was never governed directly by Constantinople, but it is impossible to separate its medieval history from Byzantium. It was the cultural capital of the world at that time. No wonder that young, emerging, neighboring states should look to it as a model.

The Serbian kingdom and its autocephalous church provided the framework for the flowering of an authentically national culture and arts. This is best evidenced in the Raska School which has given Europe notable examples of medieval architecture and painting (the monasteries of Studenica, Zica, Mileseva, Sopocani, etc). Intra-dynastic disputes, bloody at times, did not stop Serbia's growth in territorial scope, wealth, and cultural significance. Its zenith was achieved under Stefan Dusan (1331-1355).

Dusan's formative years were spent in Constantinople, during his father's exile there. He did not hide his ambitions to aspire to the throne of Byzantium. In 1345, he conquered Serres, an important city in Greece on the road to Constantinople. After several vanquishing waves southward, Dusan's authority reached from Macedonia and Albania to Epirus and Thessaly. He wanted the powerful Greek clergy in Byzantium to recognize him as their legitimate ruler. When the patriarch at Constantinople hesitated to crown him, he summoned the Serbian and Bulgarian bishops for a council at Skoplje. The bishops raised the autocephalous Serbian archbishopric of Pec to the rank of patriarchate (1346), and in less than a month the newly elected Serbian Patriarch Joanikije II crowned Stefan Dusan emperor. He may have grown up in Constantinople, but he also sought approval in the West, notably from Venice and the papacy, suggesting that he be regarded as "Captain of Christendom."

The influence of the Romanized world on Serbia was far from negligible, and at times a source of tension. In the entourage of Serbian kings, Roman Catholic courtiers, German guards, and French ladies wed to Serbian knights tried to interject aspects of Latin style, fashion, and mores. The most notable application of Romanized culture in Serbia is Stefan Decanski's (1321-1331) beautiful Monastery Church of Decani. It was built by a Franciscan friar and Dalmatian stone masons, with fresco works by artists of the Kotor school.

Most of Dusan's imperial time was spent in the Hellenic area of his realm. Speaking Greek fluently, he felt at home there, leaving central Serbia in the care of his son Uros. Dusan replaced the Greek aristocracy with Serbian administrators, his comrades in arms, and gave them Byzantine titles. But to the Roman Catholic West, Dusan remained an Eastern schismatic who was not to be trusted. Indeed, his Legal Code (*Zakonik*) further reflected his indebtedness to the Byzantine legal, political and cultural tradition.

Dusan suddenly died before he turned fifty. When his strong hand was removed, rival princes quarreled among themselves, oblivious to the growing menace of the Turks who at that time crossed into Europe and began their conquests in all directions.

Serbia of the Nemanjic dynasty was a land of economic and cultural development that surpassed the European median. It was an integral part of the international community of its time. Serbian royal courts maintained lively diplomatic relations with Venetian doges, Hungarian kings, Roman popes and Byzantine emperors. They were connected through marriage with leading courts: Stefan the First Crowned married Eudocia, daughter of Byzantine Emperor Alexis III; King Stefan Uros I married Princess Helene d'Anjou; Stefan Dragutin married Katherine, daughter of Hungarian King Stephen V...

Prince Lazar was killed at Kosovo in 1389, but Serbia lingered on for a few decades. His son Despot Stefan (1389-1427) was a dashing man of war, letters and politics, a protector of writers and artists, a humanist of wide culture, and an author in his own right. His *Ode to Prince Lazar* is chiseled on the marble column that was placed at the spot of the Kosovo Battle. In Stefan's monastery, Resava, generations of monks, scribes, and artists have preserved the Serbian heritage through the ensuing dark decades.

Stefan Lazarevic had the misfortune of presiding over the declining days of his country. Had he been Dusan's successor, instead of Lazar's, the history of the Serbian people might have been different. The respect that Stefan commanded among the Turks and Tartars at Angora, when he rode at the head of three gallant charges against Tamerlane, speaks of the effect his presence might have had if he had inherited the throne half a century earlier.

By the early 15th century the writing was on the wall. John VI Cantacuzenus could not have known what he was doing to Byzantium and to the Christian world, by inviting the support of his powerful but dangerous Muslim allies. And the countries of the West, could they have known what their insistence on ecclesiastical submission to Rome, as a price of aid, would yield? When in desperation Byzantine Emperor Manuel II begged the pope, the doge, and the kings of France, England, and Aragon for help, his plea went unanswered. Reconciliation between East and West, the Greek and the Latin worlds, Orthodoxy and Roman Catholicism, remained a vexed question throughout. The two sides did not do together what they were unable to do alone: to stop the Turks. Even the defeats at Nicopolis on the Danube in 1396 and Varna (1444), which wiped out all hopes for Christendom to clear the Balkans of the Ottoman menace, could not bring unity.

Djuradj Brankovic, the last of the Serbian despots, finally succumbed in 1459, a mere six years after Constantinople fell to the Turks. The black two-headed eagle of Byzantium moved to Moscow to become the symbol of the "Third Rome," nourishing the hopes of Balkan Slavs for centuries to come.

## THE BATTLE, IN FACT AND LORE[1]

In Serbia's medieval heyday Kosovo and Metohija was its heartland, populated by a homogenous Serbian population. This is confirmed by the many royal charters and by the recorded personal and geographic names in the area. The old toponims, names of mountains, rivers, and many towns and villages in the Province (as well as northern Albania) are of Slav origin. The very name of the region - *Kosovo and Metohija* – is derived from *kos*, blackbird, and *metoch*, Greek for "endowed church estate."

The Kosovo region is a valley surrounded by hills of some 4,200 square miles in size, with an additional 2,000 square miles of adjacent Metohija. The ancient cradle of the Serbian nation is carried by two broad-shouldered mountains, Kopaonik in the north and white-capped and Shara in the south. The hills offer excellent pastureland, while the plain is fertile and suitable for corn, wheat, fruit and wine. To those who descended from the slopes of the mountains, or who came there from poorer regions as homesteaders, Kosovo seemed a promised land. It is also a bottomless ancient mining pit, rich in zinc, lead, and silver.

Kosovo has never been a melting pot. It is a battlefield, a rendezvous for hostile earthly encounters. Byzantines, Bulgars, Magyars, Austrians, Turks, Germans, Italians,

---

1 This chapter is partly based on *The Saga of Kosovo* (East European Monographs, 1984). Used with the permission of the authors.

and NATO allies... all marched through it at certain times, but got nowhere. Kosovo was a boxing ring where world ideologies (Christian, Bogomil, Muslim, Fascist, Marxist, and postmodern) each won individual rounds, but not the fight. There have been eight major slaughters in as many centuries on this peaceful stretch of land.

Of all Kosovo battles only one counts in the formation of the psyche of a Serb. It is the one that began in the early hours of Vidovdan (St. Vitus Day, June 15, 1389 – June 28 new style). The Turks had already been on the European continent for some time, seemingly unstoppable and intoxicated by easy victories over the rival and disunited infidels. The battle took place on the part of Kosovo Plain that the Turks called Mazgit, where the rivulet Lab flows into the Sitnica River. Today's visitors learn where Sultan Murad's intestines were buried, where his standard bearer (Gazimestan) fell, and where a marble column once stood and bore the following inscription by Prince Lazar's son, Despot Stefan Lazarevic:

> *Oh man, stranger or hailing from this soil, when you enter this Serbian land, whoever you may be ... when you come to this field called Kosovo, you will see all over it plenty of bones of the dead, and with them myself in stone nature, standing upright in the middle of the field, representing both the cross and the flag. So as not to pass by and overlook me as something unworthy and hollow, approach me, I beg you, oh my dear, and study the words I bring to your attention, which will make you understand why I am standing here ... At this place there once was a great autocrat, a world wonder and Serbian ruler by the name of Lazar, an unwavering tower of piety, a sea of reason and depth of wisdom ... who loved everything that Christ wanted ... He accepted the sacrificial wreath of struggle and heavenly glory ... The daring fighter was captured and the wrath of martyrdom he himself accepted ... the great Prince Lazar ... Everything said here took place in 1389 ... the fifteenth day of June, Tuesday, at the sixth or seventh hour, I do not know exactly, God knows.*

The Serbian army in 1389 was encamped along the right bank of the Lab, an area suitable for both infantry and cavalry. Prince Lazar had many reasons to worry about the outcome of the forthcoming encounter. Murad gave him no time to rally his vassals and tributary lords, some of whom were conspicuously slow in marshaling their troops. Lazar's frantic effort to obtain help from allies such as the king of Hungary failed because it was difficult to organize help on such short notice.

Although ill-prepared, Lazar had no other choice but to face the enemy. Murad's advisers, a group of skilled military veterans, insisted on immediate action. Amassed in the area of today's Nis and Kumanovo to the east, the Turkish generals were eager to meet the Serbs while still possessing the momentum of previously victorious campaigns.

Morale in the Serbian camp was not high. Lazar's commanders were torn apart by local rivalries and distrust. Djuradj Stracimirovic-Balsic, a prince of Zeta and son-in-law of Lazar, and some vojvodas of the northern regions were delayed by local opposition. Historians are still trying to ascertain whether the revolts were real or simply used as excuses. According to chroniclers, national bards, and traditional Kosovo saga, Vuk Brankovic of the old aristocracy, who married Mara, and Milos Obilic, of lesser birth, who married Vukosava, fell prey to the ongoing feud between the two sisters.

By all accounts Prince Lazar was acutely aware that he and his people were defenders of Christendom and that the forthcoming battle would probably be the last chance for Balkan Christians to repulse the Muslims. Wise, charitable, and a skillful soldier, he defeated the Turks in encounters that took place in 1381 and 1386, but by 1389 it was becoming evident that he was winning battles but losing the war. Lazar's Bosnian ally, Tvrtko I, also beat back the Turks when they probed his domain (1386 and 1388). Initial setbacks merely made the Turks only more resolute, and in 1389 they were ready. The Eastern Christians in the Balkans were now faced not by scouting Turkish detachments but by a great army.

Sultan Murad led his army straight toward Lazar's capital Krusevac. There was a bloody assault on the fortress at Nis, which the Serbs defended for 25 days. When Murad's scouts reported the concentration of a large Serbian army at Kosovo, he marched immediately to meet it. He wanted a decisive battle that would break the backbone of Serbian resistance. According to Serbian bards and tradition, Murad sent the following message to Lazar:

> *Oh Lazar, thou head of the Serbians:*
> *There was not and never can be one land in the hands of two masters.*
> *No more can two sultans rule here …*
> *Come straight to meet me at Kosovo!*
> *The sword will decide for us.*

Modern historians face difficulties in trying to decipher the realities of the Battle of Kosovo. They have to sift through rhapsodic and idealized, mostly apologetic, renditions of relevant events. Contemporary chroniclers had to keep in mind the interest of their protectors and sponsors, with objectivity not always their trademark. But to the credit of epic writers, many provided data that were later corroborated by more reliable sources. In their rendering, Lazar sent a memorable summons to all parts of his lands:

> *Whoever born of Serbian blood or kin*
> *comes not to fight the Turks at Kosovo,*
> *To him never son or daughter born,*
> *no child to heir his land or bear his name.*
> *For him no grape grow red, no corn grow white,*
> *in his hand nothing prosper.*
> *May he live alone, unloved, and die unmourned, alone!*

Before going into battle, Lazar left the Serbian people the famous adage which they have preserved ever since, and which is the essence of the Gospel Message: *The Earthly Kingdom is short-lived, but the Heavenly One is forever.*

Murad succeeded in surprising the Serbian army, as he had done at Marica in 1371. He launched his attack early in the morning while Lazar and his commanders were at prayers in the nearby Samodreza Church. As Lazar blessed his soldiers, he led them into battle that was to decide the fate of Balkan Eastern Orthodox nations for a long period to come. The Turkish historian Neshri describes the first phase of the battle in the following words:

> *The archers of the faithful shot their arrows from both sides. Numerous Serbians stood as if they were mountains of iron. When the rain of arrows was a little too sharp for them, they began to move, and it seemed as if the waves of the Black Sea were making noise ... Suddenly the infidels stormed against the archers of the left wing, attacked them in the front, and, having divided their ranks, pushed them back. The infidels destroyed also the regiment ... that stood behind the left wing ... Thus the Serbians pushed back the whole left wing, and when the confounding news of this disaster was spread among the Turks they became very low-spirited ... Bayazet, with the right wing, was as little moved as the mountain on the right of his position (Kopaonik). But he saw that very little was wanting to lose the sultan's whole army.*

The decisiveness of the sultan's son turned the flow of the battle. Among the Turks Bayazit was known as *Ildarin* (Lightning). He attacked the flank of the advancing Serbian force and succeeded in repulsing it. At that critical moment a Serbian corps of some twelve thousand cuirassiers was supposedly withdrawn from the battle by their commander, Vuk Brankovic. Documentary evidence is scant, but he apparently either lost his nerve or thought it inadvisable to lose all of his men in a futile battle. His name, justly or not, still lives in ignominy among the Serbs as the epitome of treachery.

Lazar tried to rally his disheartened troops and led them into a new attack, but it failed. The morale of the Serbs plummeted. Wounded, Lazar was taken prisoner, and his army, falling apart, was beaten and dispersed by the early afternoon. He was beheaded only hours later in front of the mortally wounded Murad. Kneeling, he could only utter: *My God, receive my soul*. Murad lived long enough to see his enemies beheaded. As he died, his younger son Bayazet made sure immediately to eliminate his brother, Jacub, who had also taken part in the battle, and thus assure his ascendance.

As Vidovdan 1389 came to a close and the sun went down behind the mountains of in the west, the night that would last five centuries began. Two rulers lay dead on the plain of Kosovo, surrounded by their slain warriors. Murad's body was carried by his fighters all the way to Asia Minor, to the city of Bursa. Present at the burial ceremony were two Serbian nobles who were ordered by Bayazet to escort the body of their enemy, and who were executed at Murad's gravesite.

## SPIRITUAL AND POLITICAL LEGACY

The metaphysical aura surrounding the Battle of Kosovo started developing soon after the event. It is apparent in rich medieval embroidery made in 1402 in the stillness of the monastery of Ljubostinja with the needle of the pious Serbian Princess Euphemia. She sketched her requiem in gold thread on a pall to cover the severed head of Prince Lazar:

> In courage and piety did you go out to do battle against the snake Murad ... your heart could not bear to see the hosts of Ismail rule Christian lands. You were determined that if you failed you would leave this crumbling fortress of earthly power and, red in your own blood, be one with the hosts of the heavenly King ...

For the Serbs, Kosovo became a symbol of steadfast courage and sacrifice for honor, much as the Alamo for the Americans – only Kosovo was the Alamo writ large, where Serbs lost their whole nation. To them, too, in the words of Sam Houston, the site of their defeat was to be remembered, and avenged. The Serbian Orthodox Church proclaimed Prince Lazar a holy martyr. His mutilated body could not, however, rest long in his native land.[2]

Over the centuries the sacrificial courage of Prince Lazar and his army on that day in 1389 has epitomized the Hellenic and Romans dictum that it was better to die heroically than to live unfree. To the Serbs the lesson of St. Vitus Day was that eternal values must be placed before earthly ones, that spiritual force is superior to the force of arms, that by moral fortitude alone we can transcend our mortal frame and step from time into Eternity. The forces of darkness are defeated in the end and that those of light and virtue ultimately triumph – even when such victory may seem impossible – because there is God. Kosovo had redefined the Serbs as a quintessentially *Christian* nation.

The battle of Kosovo was one of the most decisive events in the whole history of Southeastern Europe. It heralded not merely the fall of the medieval Serbian state and the conquest of the whole Balkan Peninsula by a barbarous Asiatic invader, but also an important stepping stone in the struggle of Islam against Christianity.

For the next half-century the Serbs retained some fragments of their self-rule and liberty; but in 1459 their country finally became a mere province of Turkey. The nobles were exterminated. Not content with seizing their country, the Turks used vanquished Christians as the instrument of their own enslavement. One boy in five was taken away from his home and brought up as a Turk Muslim. Thus the Janissaries came into being, the famous crack regiments which made the Turks the terror of Europe.

The Turks were masters: no Christian dared ride into a town on horseback. If he failed to dismount when he met a Turk on the high road, he risked being killed upon the spot. He was not allowed to have firearms, and was at the mercy of the Turkish soldiery when they chose to plunder. A proverb which dates from those times says that *grass never grows where the hoofs of the Turkish horses once tread*. What are now fertile and prosperous valleys were in those days uncultivated and almost deserted lands. It was only in those districts which lay off the beaten track, where the soldiers and tax-collectors did not come often, that the Serbs had any chance of living peaceful and settled lives.

From 1459 to 1804 Serbia ceased to exist as a state and a self-governing nation. The nation survived on faith and on epic poetry. They turned to local bards to

---

2 As the Turks moved to the north, his remains were carried to Fruska Gora (Vrdnik Monastery) in northern Serbia. The wandering bones had to be moved a fourth time, when in 1941 the Croatian equivalent of the Nazi SS, the Ustashe, began pillaging Serbian holy places in the newly created Axis satellite, the Independent State of Croatia. Tsar Lazar's relics were taken to Belgrade for safe keeping, to rest in front of the altar of the main Orthodox cathedral. In 1989 the body of Prince Lazar was returned to the Monastery of Ravanica near Cuprija, built by himself.

keep alive the memories of their people's past glories by their ballads and tales, always with an eye to the great days which would come again and console them for the miseries of the present. Many villages had their own singer, sometimes a man gifted with the "second sight," as the bards of the Scottish Highlands of yore. In the long winter evenings the villagers gathered round them and listened to the chants, to the accompaniment of their primitive one-stringed fiddle (*gusle*), of the deeds of dead Serbian heroes. Some of the finest of these ballads centered round the thrilling incidents of the battle of Kosovo.

For centuries Serbs have celebrated the anniversary of the battle, not only as a day of mourning but as an event to be remembered and avenged. St. Vitus Day (*Vidovdan*) was a proof that for the nation, as for individuals, death is followed by resurrection. It is difficult for us to understand, in these post-modern times, how completely the story of Kosovo was bound up with the daily life of the whole Serbian nation. Perhaps the simplest proof of it is the fact that in Montenegro part of the national dress is a red cap with a black border. The black is a mourning band worn for the defeat of Kosovo and never removed, just as the battle of Flodden was mourned by all Scotland for many generations.

The battle of Kosovo meant not merely the fall of the medieval Serbian Empire and the conquest of the whole Balkan Peninsula by alien invaders, but also the triumph of Islam over Christianity in the Balkans for the ensuing 500 years. The end of the Serbian Despotate in 1459 was followed by the demise of the Kingdom of Bosnia (1463). The Ottoman Empire now ruled all Serbs, except those in the most inaccessible parts of Montenegro. Serbs, Greeks, Bulgars, Albanians and others were subjugated, their plight seemingly permanent. Some among them concluded that life would be easier if they converted to Islam. Many others decided to move out – to Hungary, or to go to the Adriatic coast, to look for a haven in Austria or in Venetian-held territories in Dalmatia. Those who stayed and did not convert were classified as *giaours*, despised infidels devoid of rights.

It took the Turks less than a century to annihilate three Christian Orthodox realms in the Balkans, divided and never assisted by Christian Western Europe. The Balkan Peninsula became a two-realm society, Muslim and Christian, one privileged and the other discriminated against. As Islamization progressed it took root better in some areas, among certain classes and in certain environments. The process was much swifter in Albanian and Bosnian lands than in Serbia's former medieval state. The Albanians did not have an autocephalous Church, and their Christianity – whether Byzantine or Latin – had not become as integral in Albanian life; it remained either

Greek or Italian. In Bosnia the widely spread *Bogomil* sect had reinterpreted the tenets of Christianity to such an extent that Islam, with its stern monotheism, appeared more acceptable than either Orthodoxy or Roman Catholicism. But to understand the implications of Islamization it would be necessary to look at the tenets of the Prophet's creed *as it is* – not as the corifei of "multiculturalism" want to portray it.

## SERBS AND ALBANIANS UNDER TURKISH RULE

The Turkish occupation did not mean the same thing for all Balkan nationalities. The Greeks, for example, who had played such an important role in the Byzantine world, were viewed with the greatest respect by the invader. The Turks were good fighters and eager to participate in the spoils of war, but when it came to bureaucracy and administration in general they were sadly lacking. It was not long after the fall of Constantinople that the city's Greek, Venetian, and Jewish communities began to bustle with activity and opulence. Someone had to provide the continuity in commerce, administration, and in understanding the affairs of the Balkan mosaic. By all standards, in the reality of the period, the Greeks were the most suited for this function. When it came to choosing who would represent the Christians and to provide spiritual leadership, the choice again fell to the Greeks. Having a Greek as Eastern Orthodox patriarch in Constantinople made a substantial difference.

A glimpse into the extremity of the situation is given by one Konstantin Mihailovic of Ostrovica  Serving for ten years as a Turkish soldier under Sultan Mehmed II he later escaped and wrote *Memoirs of a Janissary*. One of the events he described was the fall of the Serbian mining town of Novo Brdo. First the sultan ordered all gates closed except one, through which all of the inhabitants had to pass, leaving their possessions behind. *So they began passing through*, one by one, writes Mihailovic,

> *And the sultan, standing at the gate, was separating males from females*
> *... then he ordered the leaders beheaded. He saved 320 young men and*
> *704 women ... He distributed the women among his warriors, and the*
> *young men he took into the janissary corps, sending them to Anatolia.*
> *... I was there, in that city of Novo Brdo, I who write this ...*

The shipping of Christian boys to Turkish schools to become janissaries, or if talented, to be a part of the administrative apparatus, was common practice. It was part of the tribute the Christian *raya* had to pay to the Turks, but it was not always the same in all regions. Serbs were trying to hide their boys, but some of those who were taken away fared well in life. Religion, not nationality, was the fundamental factor in the Turkish concept of governance: it was possible for a *raja* child to become a grand vizier of the Turkish sultan.

Wealth and material position were important factors affecting the decision to convert. This contributed to the new stratification of the society under Ottoman rule, and a new power balance among national groups. The balance was shifting drastically in favor of the Albanians, to the detriment of good relations between them. The emergence of a significant number of Islamized Albanians holding high posts at the Porte was reflected in Kosovo and Metohija. Albanians started appearing as officials and tax collectors in local administration, replacing Turks or Arabs as the pillar of Ottoman authority. Local Serbs and Albanians, being divided first by language and culture, and subsequently by religion, gradually became members of two fundamentally opposed social and political groups.

With over thirty grand viziers of Albanian descent during Ottoman rule, the top policy-making machine was filled with people of Albanian stock. In the process of Islamization, Albanians showed themselves much more pliable than Serbs. The weight of their Albanian tradition proved a lighter burden. Theirs is the famous saying: *Ku este shpata este feja* ("Your faith is where the sword is"). Warriors fascinated by swords and guns, used to discipline and a strong hand, the Albanians represented a much better medium to be cast into the Turkish mold than the individualistic, rebellious and unpredictable Serbs.

The Albanians' readiness to come to terms with the conquerors gave them an upper hand. This was the beginning of a tragic division, of separate roads for them and for the Serbs. The former became the rulers and the latter the ruled. This parting of the ways is best seen in the deterioration of relations between neighboring Montenegrin and Albanian tribes. Living under similar conditions in the isolated highlands, having similar life patterns, traditions, and history, they were a world apart from the rest of the Balkans. They populated the roadless mountain areas that invaders had no particular desire to visit as long as their control was acknowledged by regular tax contributions and tributes. Their elected local leaders, together with their priests, ruled in strict observance of their traditions and customs. The Turkish judiciary never bothered the Christians unless Muslim rule or people were involved. Through common experiences and alliances in local conflicts, as well as opposition to outside influences, the binding word *besa* (oath, promise) often meant mutual protection.

A French traveler was taken aback, when in the late years of the 18th century he visited Herzegovina. It was the Christian holiday of St. Ilija (Elijah), but to his amazement he noticed that Muslims were going to the mosque, splendidly lit. His agitated curiosity and inquiry were given a laconic answer: *It's Ilija in the morning, Alija in the evening*! Even today one can still see Albanian Muslims of Kosovo, Metohija, or Macedonia visiting Serbian monasteries. They arrive in reverence of a saint whose icon is in the church or of relics of some Serbian king known to help where Mohammed and Esculap had failed.[3]

In the 14th and 15th centuries the great majority of Albanians were Christians, Orthodox or Roman Catholic in the north, predominately Orthodox in the south. Until some decades ago it was not unusual to see Albanians visiting with their Christian neighbors on Christian holidays, or attending weddings and baptisms. This was a legacy from the old days when the respective families were closely knit, living through periods of harmony or quarrels, but not unremitting hostility. But coexistence was severely strained by the zealous converts to the Prophet's faith. Some left a bloody trail in their forceful Islamization drive against the Serbs. An old Serbian religious inscription, made in 1574, reads: "This is where great Albanian violence took place, especially by Mehmud Begovic in Pec, Ivan Begovic in Skadar, Sinnan-Pashic Rotulovic in Prizren, and Slad Pashic in Djakovitsa - they massacred 2,000 Christians ... Have mercy upon us, Oh Lord. Look down from Heaven and free your flock."

Probably the most notorious among the converts was Koukli Bey who used force in trying to Islamize the areas of Pastrik, Has, and Opolje at the end of the 18th century. Remembered as an arch-enemy of the Serbs was another convert, Grand Vizier Sinan Pasha, who ordered the remains of Saint Sava transferred from the Mileseva Monastery to Belgrade and burned on a pyre in 1594.

The phenomenon of Islamization, and all that it meant in terms of personal welfare and social advancement, was the main cause of the estrangement between the two groups. To the Albanians, Islam was an opportunity, a vehicle not only to get even but to outrank the Greeks and the Slavs. Islamization was continuous, but its fervor and intensity were not. At certain periods, in certain areas, with certain people, the process would explode, usually triggered by some key event, like the Serbs joining the Austrian army in its incursions. The aftermath would be intensified Islamization.

The latent Serbian-Albanian conflict came into the open during the Holy League's war against the Ottoman Empire (1683-1690). Many Serbs joined the Habsburg troops as a separate Christian militia. The Albanians – with the exception of

---

3  The editor of this volume witnessed, in the summer of 1997, the arrival of an Albanian family to the walled-in monastery of *Sveti Vraci* near Orahovac, in Kosovo. They placed a sick boy (stricken by a strain of muscle-wasting disease, the abbot was told) under a coffin containing the relics of a Serb saint, and left him there overnight in the sincere conviction that the power of the Orthodox Christian martyr would help cure the young Muslim, sound asleep under his bones.

the Catholic Klimenti (*Kelmendi*) tribe – reacted in accordance with their recently acquired Islamic identity and took the side of the sultan's army against the Christians. Following the Habsburgs' defeat a huge number of local Serbs, fearing Muslim vengeance and reprisals, withdrew from Kosovo-Metohija led by their Patriarch, Arsenije III Carnojević. On their way they were joined by many people from other parts of Serbia and moved to the neighboring Habsburg Empire, to today's Vojvodina.

Two generations later yet another Austro-Ottoman war provoked further Serb migrations (1739), led by another Patriarch, Arsenije IV Jovanović-Šakabenda. Fertile farmlands thus abandoned by the Serbs in Kosovo and Metohija were gradually settled by the neighboring Muslim Albanian nomads. This settlement proceeded at a fairly slow pace at first, because the number of Orthodox Serbs who had stayed put - or who had returned after the reprisals had diminished and the situation calmed down - was still considerable. The pattern of Albanian settlement developed in uneven waves, but typically, upon the seizure of a plot of Serb-owned land, fellow tribesmen were brought in from the mountains to protect the acquisition and to help expand the considerable space needed for the herds. Thus an age-old pattern of social rivalry could be discerned: migrant herdsmen (Albanians) were in constant conflict with the settled farmers (Serbs).

This familiar pattern of social conflict was enhanced by the religious dimension. As a Muslim, an Albanian herdsman could persecute or rob a Christian Serb peasant with complete impunity. At the same time, new wars the Ottomans waged with the Habsburg Empire during the 18th century and the weakening of the central authority in Constantinople, stimulated the growth of anarchy that made the position of Christians in the Balkans increasingly intolerable. In Kosovo a process of social mimicry followed. In order to protect themselves from attacks by Muslim squatters, many Serbs accepted the outer characteristics of the Muslim Albanian population. They were obliged to accept the national costumes and language of Muslim Albanians in public communication, while they used Serbian only within their families. Less resistant Orthodox Serbs converted to Islam and afterwards, through marriages, entered Albanian clans. They were called *Arnautashi*. Their first and second generations secretly celebrated Christian feasts and retained their old surnames and customs. Eventually – and inevitably – they were assimilated into the larger group.

As for the remaining Orthodox Serbs, the religious gap between them and the Albanians in Kosovo and Metohija became the defining trait of their respective identities. It fully shaped their relations in the age of nationalism in the 19th century. The social realities were reflected at the level of religious affiliations: many Muslim Albanians considered Islam the religion of the free people, while Christianity - especially Orthodox Christianity - was the religion of slaves. The persistence of such beliefs among many Albanians was noticed by European consuls as late as the beginning of the 20th century. For many Albanians, Islam was a means for social promotion, but their ethnic identity, derived from the common tribal and patriarchal tradition, engendered far stronger loyalties and collective identities.

By the early 1800s a new factor - no less critical than ethnic or religious difference – further impeded communication between the two nations. This was the disparity in political outlook and core concepts. The Serbs had a clear idea about their statehood, while the Albanians, with occasional blips of Albanianism, were for the most part Turkish-oriented. While the Serbs dreamed of their Serbian state, the Albanians tended to identify with the Ottoman Empire of which they were a part. An early Albanian nationalist, Sami Bey Frasheri, in his history of Albania written in Turkish in 1899 and later translated into German, describes the Albano-Turkish affinity in the following words:

> *Turks were finding devout and courageous co-fighters in Albanians, while Albanians found the Turkish kind of governing very much to their taste. In Turkish times, Albania was a blossoming country because Albanians were riding together with Turks in war campaigns all over the world and were returning with rich booty: gold and silver, costly arms, and fine horses from Arabia, Kurdistan, and Hungary.*

By the early 1800s the Balkan Peninsula looked more and more like the proverbial "powder keg," and Serbia with its uprisings (1804 and 1815) was the fuse. The Serbs were soaring upward, carried on the wings of national liberation, and the Greeks were not far behind. The Albanians, pulled down by the weight of the aging Ottoman Empire, saw that the Serbs and Greeks could not be held down. They were undecided about their options.

For nine crucial years the Serbs battled the Turkish armies (1804-1813) and only two years later after being "pacified" they rose again. These two open insurrections sent shock waves throughout the Balkans and central Europe. In 1813 Karadjordje went into exile and Serbia's dream seemed crushed, but in the popular mind Karadjordje came to be viewed as the avenger of the Serbs' defeat at Kosovo as the courageous leader of the Serbs. His achievements paved the way for another attempt, and only two years later came the Second Uprising (1815), under Milos Obrenovic. He insisted on absolute obedience from his followers, and soon obtained considerable autonomy for the *pashaluk* of Belgrade (1817). A consummate politician, in his dealings with the Turks Milos combined bribes and flattery. He opened one door after another, and obtained his goals without much bloodshed.

In Milos's time the Serbs made a clear distinction between Turks and Albanians. The former were city dwellers, landholders, or artisans, while the Albanians were a sort of Muslim proletariat. Most Turks in Serbia could not come to terms with life under increasingly independent Christian rule, and moved to Turkey, but this was not the case with the Albanians. Economically, the tables were turned against the Turks: in an increasingly open society they were losing their lands, while in the cities they no longer had the monopoly on the professions. In the words of a contemporary observer, "The Turks sat grumbling, smoking their *chibuks*, drinking coffee, watching Christians taking the initiative."

Albanians, a much more aggressive segment of the Balkan Muslim world, could not just sit by and watch the Christians take over. Yet they faced with two fronts. On the one side were the Serbs, newly confident and assertive. On the other front was the Turkish "protector," who offered little protection but still imposed new restrictions and made new demands and obligations. Since Albanians were unsurprisingly unwilling to stand up to the Serbs and to Constantinople at the same time, the end of the 19th century presented them with the urgent need to develop some form of central authority to coordinate their actions. They also needed a national ideology and a national program.

With the passage of time, relations between Serbs and Albanians, instead of becoming more conciliatory, were getting worse. As the Serbian state was growing in size and political importance in Balkan affairs, Albanian fears and animosity grew apace.

## THE MODERN ERA[4]

Uneven levels of national integration among Serbs and Albanians in the age of nationalism, in the 19th and 20th centuries, gave fresh impetus to the old religious rivalries. In the Kingdom of Serbia (1912-1914), during the Great War (1914-1918), in the Kingdom of Yugoslavia (1918-1941), and during the Axis occupation (1941-1945) those conflicts were transferred into new rivalries, this time involving a strong international component related to the changed roles. Ethnic Albanians, former bearers of the Ottoman state and its religious tradition, became a minority in 1912 that was strongly antagonistic towards the state ruled by the Serbs, their former serfs. Finally, Titoist ideological manipulation invoking the national question within communist

---

4 This chapter is partly based on an essay by Dr. Dusan Batakovic. Used with the author's permission.

Yugoslavia (1945-1991), along with the constantly growing social differences, came as the final coup to every attempt at establishing inter-ethnic communication that would be based on individual, instead of on collective rights.

By the beginning of the 20th century, under the re-enthroned Karadjordjevic dynasty, Serbia took a new lease of life, and the practical proof of this was soon to be seen in the Balkan Wars of 1912 and 1913. In the first of these Serbia, in alliance with Bulgaria Greece, and Montenegro, attacked Turkey: and within one month the armies of the four Balkan allies had driven the Turks out of all their huge possessions in Europe, except little scraps of land round their capital Constantinople and round the Dardanelles. As a result all the Christians who had lived so miserably under the yoke of Turkey were set free by their own free kinsmen from across the frontiers.

Serbia needed its own port on the Adriatic coast, so that it would not have to depend on Austrian goodwill for its economic development. The natural way to this port was through Montenegro. Realizing this, Austria sought to create a political and military zone between the two Serbian states. Albanians were to play a large role in this scheme: they were to be the wall between the Montenegrins and the Serbs. This became obvious at the London Peace Conference after the Balkan War, at which the state of Albania was established.

The dawn of nationalism in the Balkans was announced by the Serbian uprising in 1804. *Die Serbische Revolution* as Leopold von Ranke called it, was characterized by the desire for the creation of a national state based on the small farmer's estate and on a democratic order derived from social background. By having stirred all the Balkan Christians, the Serbian revolution initiated an irreconcilable conflict with the Ottoman rule which the Balkan Muslims, primarily the Albanians and the Bosnian Muslims, were the first to defend.

The old religious conflict acquired a new explosive charge called nationalism. Kosovo and Metohija was ruled by renegade Albanian pashas who, like the conservative Muslim beys in Bosnia, wanted to preserve a status quo as a guarantee of their privileges. Both the Islamicized Albanians and the Bosnian Muslims persecuted the rebellious Orthodox Serbs. Simultaneously, they came into open conflict with the reform-oriented sultans who saw the salvation of the Ottoman Empire in its rapid "Europeanization."

Ever since obtaining internationally recognized autonomy (1830) the Serbs slowly but surely progressed towards the establishment of an independent nation-state according to the French model. Serbian nationalism was secularized, derived from a mixture of German Voelkisch cultural matrix based on the common language and the popular tradition, and Jacobin experiences, whose aim was to overcome the religious differences, with clear desires for liberal solutions coming from the population's social homogeneity.

Except for a certain kind of ethnic solidarity, Albanian nationalism developed under unfavorable circumstances: the tribal organization and the religious and social divisions ensured the domination of conservative layers of beys and tribal chiefs. Defending their old privileges, the Albanians, just like the Bosnian Muslims, became, in the declining Ottoman Empire, an obstacle to its modernization. Shaped by the Islamic civilizational framework the Muslim Albanians (around 70% of the entire population), were unable to successfully coordinate their privileges with the needs of modern nations. Until the Eastern Crisis (1875-1878), the Albanians moved around in a vicious circle between general loyalty to the Ottoman Empire and the defense of their local interests which meant resisting the central authorities' measures. The beginning of the Albanian national integration was therefore not based on cultural unity, and even less on liberal European-type principles.

Albanian nationalism was of an ethnic nature, but clearly burdened by conservative Islamic traditions. Simultaneously, this nationalism was more than half a century behind the other Balkan nations in defining its aspirations. The Albanians, similarly to other belated nations (verspätete nation), when confronted with rival nationalisms, sought foreign support and advocated radical solutions. In Kosovo-Metohija and in western Macedonia, where the Serbs and the Albanians were intermingled, with the system falling apart and with the growing social stagnation, it was anarchy that reigned: there the Christians were the principal victims and the Muslims were their persecutors.

The Albanian League (1878-1881), formed on the eve of the Congress of Berlin, on the periphery of the Albanian ethnic space, in Prizren, called for a resolution of the national question within the frameworks of the Ottoman Empire. Conservative Muslim groups prevailed in the League's leadership and paramilitary forces. Dissatisfied with the Porte's concessions to the European powers, the League tried to sever all ties with Constantinople; in order to prevent further international complications, the sultan Abdülhamid II (1876-1909) ordered military action and destroyed the Albanian movement.

The internationalization of the Albanian question began and, until the Balkan wars (1912-1913), it had two compatible directions. First of all, it was characterized by a renewed loyalty to the Porte due to the proclaimed pan-Islamic policy in order to encourage the Albanian Muslims to stifle Christian movements which were endangering the Ottoman empire's internal security. The persecution of and violence against the

Serbs in Kosovo-Metohija and in Macedonia were an integral part of the pan-Islamic policy of sultan Abdülhamid II. The result was at least 60,000 expelled Serbs from Old Serbia (*vilayet* of Kosovo). Refugees from Old Serbia and Macedonia sent a memorandum to the Conference in The Hague in 1899, but their complaints about systematic discrimination perpetrated by Muslim Albanians were not officially discussed.

Secondly, the Albanians, especially Roman Catholics, sought foreign support from those Powers which, in their desire to dominate the Balkans, could help Albanian aspirations. While Italy's activities among the Albanians were based on establishing influence among their Roman Catholics in the northern region and in the cities along the Adriatic coast, Austria-Hungary had more ambitious plans. After the occupation of Bosnia-Herzegovina (1878), the Dual Monarchy planned to penetrate further into the Balkans, towards Salonika. For Vienna the Albanians in Kosovo-Metohija and western Macedonia were a bridge towards the Vardar river valley.

The slowness of the Albanians national integration was favorable to a broad action by the Dual Monarchy: the Albanian élite, divided among three religious communities, just like the nation itself, consisted of people of unequal social statuses speaking different dialects. In order to overcome the existing differences, Vienna launched important cultural initiatives. Books about Albanian history were printed and distributed, national coats-of-arms were invented and various grammars were written in order to create a unified Albanian language. The Latin script, supplemented with new letters for non-resounding sounds, was envisaged as the common script.

The most important cultural initiative was the "Illyrian theory" about the Albanians' origin. The theory about the Albanians' alleged Illyrian origin was launched from the cabinets of Viennese and German scientists where, until then, it only had the form of a narrow scientific debate, and it was skillfully propagated in a simplified form. According to this theory, for which reliable scientific evidence has not been found to the present day, the Albanians are the oldest nation in Europe created through a mixture of pre-Roman Illyrian and Pelasgian tribes from an Aryan flock (Volksschwarm). Thus, a hugely questionable scientific thesis about the ethno-genesis of a nation was turned into the mythological basis for national integration, which - in the fullness of time - became the main pillar of the Albanians' modern national identity and the basis for their territorial aspirations.

The way in which Vienna used the Albanian national movement against the "Greater Serbian danger" in its conflict with the Serbian movement for unification, was similar to the way in which Russia tried to manipulate the Serbian question, during the Serbian revolution, in its wars with Turkey. But the results were different. The

Serbs successfully got rid of Russia's tutelage creating, with many difficulties, a modern parliamentary state (1888-1894,1903-1914) that conducted its own independent national policy; the Albanians got from Vienna an important framework for further cultural emancipation but its price was a permanent rivalry with Serbia and Montenegro. Although deeply distrustful towards the Albanian movement, both Serbian kingdoms tried, on several occasions, to establish cooperation with the Albanian leadership and to resolve mutual disputes without the interference of the Great Powers. The support to the Albanian insurrections against the Young Turk pan-Ottoman policy (1910-1912), prior to the liberation of Kosovo (1912), were obvious expressions of such efforts.

A major problem for the Albanians, in terms of national ideas, was that they were divided into three distinct segments: those in the interior regions, those on the periphery, and those living abroad. Those in the interior were very conservative; they deeply distrusted their compatriots abroad; they believed firmly in Muslim solidarity (with the Turks); and they nursed a degree of animosity toward their Christian compatriots or who were susceptible to Latin, Slav, or Greek influences. They lived insulated in their feudal mentality, which meant that a few more decades would be needed before they would be ready for the nationalist "yeast" that was working so well in the border regions. Hence, the interior and the periphery were poles apart - while those living abroad were insistent in seeking to take the reins of the national awakening movement.

It is perhaps understandable why the Albanian patriots found it necessary to start the national "awakening" process in the border regions, where the mentality was somewhat less conservative, if not rather radical. These regions, as a rule, experienced some Greek and Slav influences. This may explain why Bitolj, Ohrid, Kicevo, Debar, Prizren, Pristina, Djakovica, and Skadar attracted the "revolutionaries." There was a definite philosophical affinity between the outsiders and border region Albanians.

Turkish administration had contributed greatly to that affinity. When setting up multinational areas under their rule into *vilayets* (districts), the Turks purposely drew the dividing lines in such a way so as to encompass several nationalities in a district, instead of separating them. Whatever the rationale for such a policy, it kept rivalry alive and prevented a common front against the Turks. The Albanian leaders were aware of Turkish perfidy. The first point of their national demands insisted on "Albania to be constituted as a single vilayet." The difficulty with this was that the four districts demanded by the Albanians, as drawn by Turkish administrators, included numerous Greeks, Serbs, and Bulgarians.

When in 1912, Serbia, Greece, Montenegro, and Bulgaria declared war on Turkey, neither Austria nor the Albanians were ready for the Balkan blitz. Certain Serbian emissaries had talked with some Albanian leaders, exploring the possibilities of joining in an insurgency against the Turks. But the Albanians could not at that time fathom the military weaknesses of the Turkish army, so they stayed aloof. Most of them were against the Young Turks, but not Turkey; when the Young Turks consented not to push reforms, Albanian animosity was appeased. Albanian unrestricted violence against the defenseless Serbian population in Kosovo and elsewhere, in the period 1903-1912, had made them overconfident. They murdered the Russian consul in Mitrovica with impunity. Serbian consuls in the area were sending back reports that sounded like real horror stories, and the Serbian premier, Nikola Pasic, deplored the "difficult situation facing the Serbs in the area." Turkish authorities were either unable or unwilling to stop the Albanian harassment of Serbs.

When informed of rumors about an Albanian assault on Prizren, many local Turks began packing and heading south for safer cities. Everything pointed to total chaos, which culminated in the massive march of some 15,000 Albanians on Skoplje (August 12, 1912). Even when earlier Sultan Mehmed V himself came to Kosovo, Albanians, enraged by the Turkish reforms, were not listening anymore. Armed Albanian units occupied Djakovica, Mitrovica, and finally entered Skoplje. And Turkey, in a state of political transition, felt that action against the Albanian insurgents could wait. In the meantime, the Balkan powers had moved swiftly in their war against the Ottoman Empire.

The Serbs defeated the Turks at Kumanovo (October 23, 1912), and met with the Montenegrin forces in Metohija (October 29). The Montenegrins liberated Pec and Djakovica, while the Serbian army entered Pristina and Prizren. Kosovo was free! And one of Vienna's prime aims in the Balkans, the prevention of a common border between Serbia and Montenegro had been nullified. When Serbia realized that there was an opportunity to reach the sea, the army was ordered to cross the river Drim. It pushed through Albania, entering the cities of Ljes, Kroja, and Tirana. On November 29th the Serbian cavalry waded into the Adriatic, and took the port of Drac. The Albanians, during this sweep, fought in the ranks of the Turkish army. As the situation at the front worsened, however, they started to trickle off and desert.

As the news from the front began reaching the capital cities, the Great Powers were surprised, but Vienna was stunned. The German General Staff took it as a personal humiliation, because the top Turkish officers were their pupils. Francis Ferdinand in Vienna called the Serbs "a bunch of thieves, murderers, no-goods, and hooligans," as Vienna was preparing for a diplomatic denial of Serbia's achievements. Top leaders among Albanian nationalists (Ismail Kemal, Faik Konitza, Fan Noli, and others) were caught unprepared for the Turkish defeat. Overnight all Albanian eyes turned toward Vienna, the only possible savior by virtue of the diplomatic and military power it could wield.

The London Conference of Ambassadors was called (December 17, 1912) to decide on Albanian frontiers, and on the withdrawal of the occupation forces. The future of the victorious Serbian exploit did not seem bright. Austria-Hungary, which had been surprised by the Balkan powers' swift action, was adamant. It insisted on a Serbian pullout, and the creation of a separate Albanian unit. The Conference of Ambassadors decided on the "creation of an autonomous Albania, under the sovereignty and suzerainty of the sultan and under the exclusive guarantee of the six Great Powers." In the spring of 1913, *independence* was substituted for "autonomy," and Austria-Hungary and Italy were entrusted with the task of working it out. By the end of July 1913 the ambassadors finally decided it would need a body of "six plus one" (six representatives of the Great Powers and one Albanian) to set up the new administration. German Prince Wilhelm von Wied was chosen to become "hereditary prince of Albania," but he did not stay long enough to get to know his subjects. He left in a hurry, as soon as he learned that Francis Ferdinand was felled by a shot of a young Serbian nationalist in Sarajevo.

A great deal of squabbling, tense dispute, and hard-driving give-and-take took place during the months (1913) of the London ambassadorial meetings. The participants agonized over the death of Turkey, the birth of Albania, and the demands of the Balkan allies. Neither the Serbs nor the Montenegrins worried too much about the form of the Albanian state, or its status. As far as they were concerned, creating an independent state in their immediate neighborhood was a blessing. It was always better to have a small, hopefully reasonable, nation at your border than an insatiable imperialistic Great Power, be it Italy, Turkey, or Austria-Hungary. The main concern of the Serbs was the boundary lines, and a convenient outlet to the sea. When it became clear that they would be deprived of the latter, the Serbian team concentrated on the boundary line.

As far as the Albanians were concerned, if they had to choose between living in Slav Serbia or Muslim Turkey, they would always opt for Turkey. In what form, system, or arrangement was of secondary importance. It was a reverse of the Serbian strategy in the previous century. When Prince Milos was in a similar situation, he first attended to whatever form of national assertion was possible, leaving geography for later.

Before the curtain fell on Serbia and Montenegro the two small brothers showed the world what hearts beat in them. On July 28, 1914, Austria-Hungary declared war on Serbia. Old Pasic was eating his lunch in a local pub when the courier brought him the sealed envelope. His only comment to a bystander was: "This is the end of Austria. Lord Almighty will help us to come out winners."

## SERBIAN-ALBANIAN RELATIONS BETWEEN THE WARS

As the end of World War I approached, and Serbia inched ever nearer to the fulfillment of its war aim - the unification of all South Slavs in one independent state - relations with Albanians took a new turn. Their mighty protector and the main instigator of anti-Serbian attitudes in the area, Austria-Hungary, was about to leave the historical scene. It was about to be replaced by Italy, which had the support of the West – which Vienna did not have. The Entente had made numerous promises to Italy in the Secret Treaty of London (1915), and Italy wasted no time in seeking to achieve its objectives.

In Versailles in 1919 the newly-created Yugoslav state was among the few voices among the allies pleading for an independent Albania, free of any Great Power patronage. This position was markedly different from the Italian view. Italy, which had begun with an interest in the Albanian littoral, now wanted half of Albania and was pushing the Great Albania concept, which meant the incorporation of Serbian lands, such as Kosovo, into the new Albanian state. Belgrade's position on Kosovo was not negotiable and had not changed since the discussions at the London Conference of Ambassadors ( January 1913): Serbia could not allow the Kosovo area to be a "malignant tumor." In addition, Serbia never considered Kosovo as small change or a bargaining chip to be used by diplomats at the negotiating table.

The historic, cultural, and moral reasons which guided Belgrade in opposing foreign pretensions to Kosovo were fully presented to the London meeting in 1913, and did not change in 1919 in the Royal Yugoslav format. They are just as valid today, eight decades later, although in a diametrically different ideological context. The memorandum submitted by Serbia's delegates to the 1913 conference, read in part:

> *Today the majority in those areas are Arnauts [Albanians], but from the middle of the 14th century until the end of the 17th century that land was so pure Serbian ... that the Serbs established their Patriarchate in Pec ... and near Pec is the Serbian monastery, Decani, the most famous monument of Serbian architecture and piety from the 14th cen-*

*tury. It is impossible to imagine that [these] would have been built in a region in which the Serbian people were not in a majority. The region in which are found Pec, Djakovica, and Decani, is the most holy among all Serbian lands. It is impossible to imagine any Montenegrin or Serbian government which would be in a position to yield that land to Arnauts or to any- one else ... On that question the Serbian people cannot and will not yield, nor enter into any agreements or compromises, and therefore the Serbian government is not in a position to do so.*

The moral impact that the liberation of Kosovo had as a fulfillment of Serbia's historic mission was tremendous. Western diplomats had difficulty understanding this. Operating in societies where traditional values are, if necessary, also negotiable, they viewed Serbia's history in terms of "progress" made in a brief span of time. They could not understand the uncompromising position of the Serbs when it came to losing a few cities here and there compared to the overall national advantage gained in only a few years. The "some you lose, some you win" philosophy could not be applied to Kosovo. Serbia just could not accept the Entente's concept of giving certain Serbian lands to Serbia in exchange for giving other equally historic Serbian lands to someone else.

European diplomatic big guns like Lloyd George (who in 1919 said, "I've got to polish off Pashich") and British public opinion molders such as Wickham Steed and R. W. Seton-Watson, were plainly annoyed with Serbia's stubbornness. Once again, the Serbs had an image problem in Western Europe. The Serbian Government could not get rid of the burden which history has placed upon her shoulders - the prejudice in Western Europe about the historic mission of Serbia, which is to open the door to the Russians in the south of Europe ... Britain viewed Serbia exclusively from that perspective.

Following World War I, Rome continued with its old practice of stirring Serbo-Albanian conflicts, now as a function of the conflict with the newly established Kingdom of Serbs Croats and Slovenes (renamed Yugoslavia in 1929) over dominance of the eastern Adriatic coast. Kosovo-Metohija was an unquiet border province where Albanian outlaws (kaçaks) and activists of the Kosovo Committee, an organization of emigrants which, in its struggle for a "Greater Albania," was financed by the Italian government. In Yugoslavia, like in pre-war Serbia, the ethnic Albanians were a minority that was antagonistic towards the state ruled by their former serfs. The Kosovo beys, who led the ethnic Albanians, were happy to strike deals with Belgrade on their privileges.

Belgrade responded with twofold measures: on the internal level, it carried out a recolonization of Serbs in Kosovo in order to restore the demographic structure disrupted in the last decades of Ottoman rule and tried to establish security by severe military and police means in the region bordering on Albania; for this reason the colonists were the victims of retaliation carried out by ethnic Albanian outlaws. On the foreign level, the Kingdom of Yugoslavia reacted by actively interfering in the internal political clashes in Albania and by helping to organize the liquidation of the most prominent ethnic Albanian emigrants from Kosovo like Bairam Curri and Hasan Prishtina, but without the strength to have a decisive influence on Tirana.

What happened in Kosovo after World War I was not just a "change of occupiers," the Serbian master replacing the Turkish one, as some Albanians like to portray it. The fact is that, after centuries of social immobility, Kosovo suddenly went through a revolutionary change The Serbian liberation of Kosovo, in a small way, resembled the Napoleonic push through Europe. It opened many doors to the Albanians. That they were unable or unwilling to use them is another matter.

One of the most unfortunate things for the Albanian masses of Kosovo was their being abandoned by their leaders. As if that was not enough, these same leaders instigated Kosovo Shiptars to act against the Yugoslav authorities. The mushrooming of "committees for the liberation of Kosovo," in Albania and elsewhere, resulted in the sending of terrorists and irredentist literature into the Kosovo area, sometimes allied with Bulgarian, Croatian, Hungarian, and Comintern terrorists. In spite of such activity, an increasing number of Kosovo Albanians began to realize that accommodation, if not assimilation, was the most reasonable course to follow.

In the main, Serbian political parties took Kosovo seriously, seeing in it an opportunity to fill a vacuum and thereby collect some votes before others gained this support. The leading Radical Party, the strong Democratic Party, the broadly based agricultural bloc, and the Communist Party - all showed up in Kosovo. Already in 1919, the Kosovo Albanians formed their own political organization, called *Dzemijet*. They held their annual congresses, published the group's paper *Moudjaeda* (Struggle), and conducted a variety of cultural programs. In the November 1920 elections Dzemijet elected eight deputies; in March 1923 this number grew to 18. Later the membership split, as many found that the strong and influential Serbian parties were of greater benefit and more likely to deliver. By the end of 1925, Dzemijet went out of existence, and the former members either joined the pro-government coalition groups or the opposition coalition.

Joining a Serbian party did not, however, mean conversion, as later developments would show. In 1941, many of those who had joined Serbian parties became protagonists of the Greater Albania under Italian occupation. They were the ones that Italian foreign minister, Count Ciano, in 1939 called "daggers pointed at Yugoslavia's back."

The Albanian minority in Yugoslavia, thanks to its myopic leadership, made two blunders at the very beginning. Rebellious, it chose the wrong ally; introvert, it locked itself in its own cocoon. Even when in the 1930s it became obvious that Albanians had already begun to participate in Yugoslav day-to-day reality - culturally, professionally, and politically - the residue of the unfortunate 1918 beginning was still noticeable. Perhaps there were too many people around who would not let it be forgotten. To let the forgetting take place required a longer span of time than the 20 years of the first Yugoslavia. When World War II came, the bedlam started all over again.

On the eve of that war, on January 21, 1939, Count Ciano and Yugoslav premier Milan Stojadinovic conferred in Belgrade about the "Albanian question." Stojadinovic was told of Italy's intention to occupy Albania, and apparently was promised Skadar in return, as well as the cessation of anti-Yugoslav propaganda with regard to Kosovo. A few days earlier, King Zog had received an Italian plan - in effect an ultimatum - for a reorganization of the state, which amounted to a loss of independence and practical annexation. With 30,000 Italian troops landing at four Albanian ports, Zog fled, and the Albanian parliament offered the Albanian crown to Victor Emmanuel III. In the meantime, Stojadinovic had resigned, and Ciano felt no obligation to his successor.

The Italian occupation was humiliating to many Albanians, but the Kosovo Albanians felt encouraged by it. Their dream of a Great Albania was to become a reality - after the fall of Yugoslavia in 1941 - even if under the aegis of the Italian crown. After Yugoslavia's defeat in the April war of 1941, its territories were granted to a number of satellite pro-Nazi states. Kosovo and part of western Macedonia were annexed, as compensation, to an Albania which was from 1939 under Italian occupation.

The immediate consequence of the creation of Mussolini's Greater Albania was the merciless persecution and expulsion of around 100,000 Serbs, while over ten thousand were the victims of the punitive actions of various Albanian militias. In the same period, around 75,000 people moved to Kosovo from Albania. New persecutions of the Serbs followed the capitulation of Italy (1943), when Kosovo fell under the direct control of the Third Reich. The Albanians in Kosovo wholeheartedly supported their new masters, which was reflected in the creation of the Nazi-sponsored "Second

Albanian League." Thousands of young Albanians enthusiastically enlisted in the SS "Skenderbeg" division. and embarked on a new wave of violence against the remaining Serbian civilian population.

## KOSOVO UNDER TITO AND HIS SUCCESSORS

The attempt to achieve a historical reconciliation of the Serbs and Albanians within the framework of the new social project - Soviet-type communism - proved to be impossible: the geopolitical realities remained unchanged, while the old rivalry over territories only acquired a new ideological framework.

Tito, in seeking to win over the Albanians of Kosovo during his wartime struggle to seize power, led them to believe that after the war they would have the right of self-determination, including the right of secession. But his decision at the end of the war to make Kosovo-Metohija an autonomous unit within Serbia was not warmly received. Nevertheless, several other actions of the Tito regime began to change the character of Kosovo-Metohija rather radically in favor of the Albanians. Some 100,000 Serbs were forced out of Kosovo during World War II, and they were not permitted to return. Moreover, with each passing year, more and more Serbs were forced to leave, between 150,000 and 200,000 in the 20-year period 1961-1981 alone. In the meanwhile, immediately after the war, over 200,000 Albanians were brought in from Albania to Kosovo region - and over the years Kosovo Albanians gained increasing control over events in the province.

Realpolitik forced communist ruler J.B.Tito to preserve Yugoslavia's integrity in order to become its legal successor. Simultaneously, he had to take into account the feelings of the Serbs, the communists and partisans who constituted the majority of his forces. The ethnic Albanian rebellion against communist Yugoslavia at the beginning of 1945 intensified the need for Kosovo-Metohija to remain part of Serbia, within the new Soviet type federal system. But even this solution was only tentative. The project of a Balkan federation which, apart from Yugoslavia and Albania, was also to include Bulgaria, and where Kosovo would, in accordance with Tito's idea, belong to Albania, had a twofold meaning. For Tito it was the achievement of his personal ambition to become the ruler of the Balkans reshaped into a Balkan federation under his rule. On the other hand, for communist leader of Albania Enver Hohxa this was an attempt to achieve Kosovo's annexation to Albania through mutual agreement between communist "brethren". The severance of relations with Albania in 1948, done as part of Yugoslavia's conflict with the Cominform, stopped the second wave of the immigration of ethnic Albanians into Yugoslavia favored by the Tito's government in order to obtain further influence on Albania. The number of those immigrants has not been precisely determined to the present day.

Decreeing the creation of new nations immediately after 1945 - first the Macedonians (by using linguistic criteria) and Montenegrins (by state tradition), and then also the Bosnian Moslems by religious criteria (1968) was aimed at reversing the political and military domination of the Serbs in the Kingdom of Yugoslavia. According to Milovan Djilas, one of Tito's closest aides at that time, the division of Serbs in five out of the six republics was aimed at diminishing the "centralism and hegemonies of the Serbs", as one of the main "obstacles" to the establishment of communism.

In communist Yugoslavia, the Serbo-Albanian conflicts were only part of the complex concept for resolving the national question which was carried out in phases and in the name of "brotherhood and unity" by Josip Broz Tito. Being a Croat, brought up in the Habsburg milieu marked by the fear of "the Greater Serbian danger" and on Lenin's teaching that the nationalism of big nations is more dangerous than the nationalism of smaller ones, Tito was consistent in stifling any manifestation of "the Greater Serbian hegemony" which, according to the communists, was personified in the regimes of the Kingdom of Yugoslavia.

The first two decades of bureaucratic centralism (1945-1966) were necessary for the communist leadership to avoid the debate on genocide perpetrated against the Serbs during the civil war. The centralism also aimed to consolidate communist power: during that period Tito relied on Serbian cadres (Aleksandar Rankovic) with whom he emerged victorious from the civil war. Among the victims of the State security service (UDBA), headed by Rankovic, as ideological enemies there were Serbs and ethnic Albanians alike. Together with ethnic Albanians who were persecuted for supporting former Balli Kombetar nationalist forces (actions of confiscating guns), the Kosovo-Metohija Serbs, especially Orthodox priests, were constantly arrested and monastic properties destroyed or confiscated. The biggest Orthodox Church in Metohia, built in Djakovica in the1920s was demolished in 1950, and in its place a monument for Kosovo-Metohija partisans was erected.

The decentralization based on the plans of Tito's closest associates, Edvard Kardelj - a Slovene, autnor of almost all the Yugoslav constitutions, and Vladimir Bakaric - a Croat, aimed at strengthening the competencies of the federal units, led to the renewal of nationalisms. The creation of the national-communism formulated by Edvard Kardelj as party ideology was directly promoted by Tito himself. National communism made republican and provincial parties the bearers of the national and state sovereignty. National homogenization was imposed, a process that in Kosovo-Metohija took the direction of creating a national state of the Muslim Albanians. Endeavors to create nation-states in areas marked by republican (and in the case of Kosovo-Metohija also provincial) boundaries, was also the beginning of the ethnic and religious discrimination of minority nations within the federal (provincial) entities.

National-communism which emerged in Slovenia, Croatia, Macedonia and Kosovo in the late 1960's and early 1970's was supported by Tito in order to preserve his undisputed authority challenged by the reform-orientated 'liberals' in Serbia. In the last phase of Tito's rule, marked by the (con)federal Constitution of 1974, he became, similar to Leonid Brezhnev in the USSR, the main obstacle to any further liberal evolution of the system.

As Tito's only legacy there remained the common, but ideological army, and the bulky party-bureaucratic apparatus, divided along republican and provincial borders. Those borders, although allegedly administrative, increasingly resembled the borders of self-sufficient, covertly rival national states, linked from the inside only by the iron authority of the charismatic leader. The important cohesive element on the international plane was a common fear of a potential Soviet invasion.

Within such a context, Kosovo-Metohija had an important role: first it was an autonomous region (1946 Constitution), then an autonomous province within Serbia (1963 Constitution) and finally an autonomous province only formally linked with Serbia (Constitutional amendments 1968-1971 and 1974 Constitution). Kosovo's competencies were hardly any different from those of the republics, although the Leninist principle concerning the right to self-determination was reserved for the republics only. Kosovo owed the change of its status within the federation not to the freely expressed will of the people of Serbia - Serbs and ethnic Albanians alike - but exclusively to the ideological concepts of a narrow circle of national-communist hardliners around Tito.

After the reconciliation with Moscow (1955) and the gradual normalization of relations with Albania (1971), Tito favored the ethnic Albanians in Kosovo. His Communist apparatchiks in Pristina of Albanian nationality saw this as a long awaited opportunity for a historical revenge against the Serbs. The erasing of the name of Metohija, as a Serbian Orthodox term, from the name of the autonomous province (autumn 1968), symbolically indicated the political direction of the ethnic Albanian communist *nomenklatura* in Kosovo.

What began as the "Autonomous Kosovo-Metohija Region" (1947), became the "Autonomous Province of Kosovo and Metohija" (1963), and ended up as the "Socialist Autonomous Province of Kosovo" (1969). These may seem to be insignificant semantics, but under Yugoslav conditions it meant ascending from a faceless geographic entity to a "constituent element of the federation." The 1969 formula was subsequently used by the Albanians to demand the status of a republic in the Yugoslav Federation, which could in turn lead to the riddance of Serbia's tutelage. This dawned upon the Serbian Communists only later, when the statistics on the rapidly growing Albanian majority became alarming. In 1946 the Albanians made up about 50 percent of the population of Kosovo, but by 1981 it was 77.5 percent. The corresponding percentage for Serbs and Montenegrins had dropped to about 15 percent (Yugoslav statistics list Serbs and Montenegrins separately). Thus, as the Albanian goal of an ethnically pure Kosovo almost turned into a reality, that reality became increasingly unbearable for those who could not pack up and leave.

After 1969 Kosovo got its own supreme court and its own Albanian flag. Belgrade University extension departments at Pristina were upgraded to the level of an independent university. This is when the leaders of Pristina's youth turned away from Belgrade and toward Ti,ana. Belgrade could not provide either Albanian teachers or Albanian textbooks. Tirana was more than glad to oblige. In 10 years (1971-1981) it sent to Kosovo 240 university teachers, together with textbooks written in the Albanian literary language. At the same time came the aggressive folklore that Shukrija was talking about: Albanian historic and socialist movies, Albanian TV and radio, and sport and cultural exchange visits.

Economically, Kosovo was moving ahead. With 8 percent of the Yugoslav population, it was allocated up to 30 percent of the Federal Development Funds. The Kosovo authorities, it was discovered later, used large sums from these funds to buy up land from Serbs and give it to Albanians. Investment loans were given for periods as long as 15 years, with a 3 year grace period and an interest rate of a mere 3 percent. Kosovo, always considered 1 of the "underdeveloped" areas of Yugoslavia, now received priority treatment. In a five-year period in the 1970s, for instance, some 150 million dollars were pumped into it annually. Moreover, of one billion dollars of World Bank development credit to Yugoslavia, Kosovo got 240 million, or 24 percent. It is estimated that in the 1980s some 2,1 billion dollars had been poured into the Kosovo economy. Much of the cultural support, social services, and educational aid were never to be repaid.

In view of all that aid, it is often asked why Kosovo persistently lagged so far behind other parts of the federation. Why was it among the poorest regions of Yugoslavia? Demographic reasons are usually cited, the Kosovo area having a birth rate of 32 per 1,000 (the highest in Europe), and the largest families (6.9 members). Other explanations given included Albanian backwardness, lack of management skills, corruption, investing in unproductive prestige enterprises, unrealistic and over-ambitious planning.

Tito's death on May 4, 1980 ushered in a long period of political instability, worsened by growing economic crisis and nationalist unrest. This became apparent in the streets of Pristina in March 1981, when Albanian students rioted over long queues in their university canteen. This seemingly trivial dispute rapidly spread throughout Kosovo and took on the character of a national revolt, with massive popular demonstrations in many Kosovo towns. The protesters demanded that Kosovo should become the seventh republic of Yugoslavia. The Communist Yugoslav presidency quelled the disturbances by sending in riot police and the army and proclaiming a state of emergency, although it did not repeal the province's autonomy as some Serbian leaders demanded. CPY hardliners instituted a fierce crackdown on nationalism of all kinds, Albanian and Serbian alike.

Tension between the Albanian and Serbian communities continued to escalate. The Belgrade media reported that Serbs and Montenegrins were being persecuted. The worsening state of Kosovo's economy made the province a poor choice for Serbs seeking work. Albanians tended to favor their compatriots when employing new recruits. Kosovo was the poorest part of Yugoslavia: in 1979 the average per capita income was $795, compared with the national average of $2,635 (and $5,315 in Slovenia).

It was against this tense background that the Serbian Academy of Sciences and Arts conducted a survey under Serbs who had left Kosovo in 1985 and 1986. The report concluded that a considerable part of those who had left had been under pressure by Albanians to do so. At the same time, sixteen prominent members of the SANU began work in June 1985 on a draft document that was leaked to the public in September 1986. The SANU Memorandum, as it has become known, focused on the political difficulties facing Serbs in Yugoslavia, pointing to Tito's deliberate hobbling of Serbia's body-politic and the difficulties faced by Serbs outside Serbia.

The Memorandum paid special attention to Kosovo, arguing that the province's Serbs were being subjected to "physical, political, legal and cultural genocide" in a war that had been ongoing since the spring of 1981. The Memorandum's authors claimed that 200,000 Serbs had moved out of the province over the previous twenty years and warned that there would soon be none left "unless things change radically." The remedy, according to the Memorandum, was for "genuine security and unambiguous equality for all peoples living in Kosovo and Metohija [to be] established" and "objective and permanent conditions for the return of the expelled [Serbian] nation [to be] created." It concluded that "Serbia must not be passive and wait and see what the others will say, as it has done so often in the past."

The Albanians saw the Memorandum as a call for Serbian supremacy at a local level. They claimed that all Serb emigrants had left Kosovo for economic reasons. Other Yugoslav ethnic groups—notably the Slovenes and Croats—saw a threat in the call for a more assertive Serbia. Serbs themselves were divided: the Communist old guard strongly attacked the Memorandum's message. One of those who denounced it was a Serbian Communist Party official named Slobodan Milošević.

## THE MILOSEVIC ERA

The Serbs' growing national frustration was skillfully used, after a party coup in 1987, by Milosevic, the new leader of the Serbian communists. Instead of party forums he used populist methods, taking over from the Serbian Orthodox Church and the liberal intelligentsia the role of the protector of national interests. Milosevic's intention to renew the weary communist party on the basis of new national ideals (as did the national-communist in other republics more than a decade earlier), was opposite to the movement in Eastern Europe where an irreversible process of communism's demise by means of nationalism was launched. At that moment, for most of the Serbs preoccupied by the Kosovo question, the interests of the nation were more important than the democratic changes in Eastern Europe, especially since Milosevic had created the semblance of the freedom in the media and former historical and ideological taboos were freely discussed. Democracy in Serbia was blocked in the late 1980s by the unresolved national question.

Most Albanians responded with a series of strikes and demonstrations, aware that the abolition of the autonomy based on the 1974 Constitution meant the abolition of Kosovo's budding statehood. Their actions only strengthened Milosevic position as the Serb national leader. The support of Slovenia and later on Croatia for the Albanians merely cemented Milosevic's charisma. An old dispute over land became seemingly ideological: Serbia, thanks to Milosevic, acquired the false image of "the last bastion of communism in Europe," while the Albanians obtained the halo of Western-approved victimhood in their supposed search for democracy and human rights.

The secessionist movement of the Albanians in Kosovo, derived from the logic of the Titoist order and based on ethnic intolerance, led to the homogenization of the Serbs in Yugoslavia, thus directly producing Milosevic, the neo-communist quasi-nationalist. This resulted in the homogenization of the other Yugoslav nations. In a country with such volatile mixture, ethnic mobilization directly led to the civil war. The violent disintegration of Yugoslavia in 1991-1999 was the belated revenge of Tito and his ideological heirs.

Milosevic took the process of retrenchment a stage further in 1990 when he revoked the aspects of Kosovo's and Vojvodina's autonomy and replaced locally chosen leaders with his sympathizers. As both provinces had a vote in the eight-member Yugoslav Presidency, this gave Milosevic an automatic four votes. Slovenia, Croatia, Bosnia and Macedonia thus had to maintain an uneasy alliance to prevent Milosevic from driving through constitutional changes. Serbia's political changes were ratified in a 5 July 1990 referendum across the entire republic of Serbia, including Kosovo. A new curriculum was imposed in all higher education institutions in Kosovo – a move which was rejected by Albanians who responded by creating their parallel education system.

With Kosovo's communist party effectively broken up by Milosevic, the dominant Albanian group became the Democratic League of Kosovo of Ibrahim Rugova. He called on the Albanian populace to boycott the Yugoslav and Serbian states by not participating in any elections, by ignoring the military draft and by not paying any taxes. He also called for the creation of parallel Albanian schools, clinics and hospitals.

On April 22, 1996, four attacks on Serbian security personnel were carried out simultaneously in several parts of Kosovo. A hitherto unknown organization calling itself the Kosovo Liberation Army (KLA) subsequently claimed responsibility. The nature of the KLA was at first mysterious. Initially it was a small, mainly clan-based and not well organized group of radicalized Albanians, many of whom came from the Drenica region of western Kosovo. But the KLA received financial and material support from the Kosovo Albanian diaspora and from Albanian drug lords in Europe. In early 1997, Albania collapsed into chaos following the fall of President Sali Berisha. Military stockpiles were looted with impunity by criminal gangs, with much of the hardware ending up in western Kosovo and so boosting the growing KLA arsenal.

In 1998 the U.S. State Department listed the KLA as a terrorist organization. The Republican Policy Committee of the U.S. Senate complained of the "effective alliance" of the Clinton administration with the KLA due to "numerous reports from reputable unofficial sources (...) that the KLA is closely involved with: the extensive Albanian crime network (...) [and with] terrorist organizations motivated by the ideology of radical Islam, including assets of Iran and of the notorious Osama Bin Laden."

Neither the United States nor the other influential powers made any serious effort to stop money or weapons being channeled into Kosovo. Meanwhile, the U.S. held an outer wall of sanctions against Yugoslavia which had been tied to a series of issues,

Kosovo being one of them. These were maintained despite the agreement at Dayton to end all sanctions. The Clinton administration claimed that Dayton bound Yugo-slavia to hold discussions with Rugova over Kosovo. By early 1998 Western diplomats insisted that Serbia and Yugoslavia be responsive to Albanian demands.

A decade later a far more astute American diplomat, former U.S. Ambassador to the United Nations John Bolton, warned that "Kosovo will be a weak state suscep-tible to radical Islamist influence from outside the region... a potential gate for radical-ism to enter Europe," a stepping stone toward an anti-Christian, anti-American "Eura-bia." His was a rare voice in Washington to warn of the ongoing merger of aggressive greater-Albanian nationalism and transnational Islamism. But the symbiosis between the KLA, Kosovo's Albanian crime families and the Jihadist networks abroad has its roots in the events of 1998.

While an intricate Islamic terror network was maturing in Bosnia, Osama bin Laden found fresh Balkan opportunities in Kosovo, but the Clinton Administration ignored the warnings. Iran also supported the Albanian insurgency in Kosovo, hoping to turn the region into their main base for Islamic armed activity in Europe. By the end of 1998, with Bin ᵀ aden's network firmly established in Albania, the U.S. drug officials (DEA) complained that the transformation of the KLA from terrorists into freedom fighters hampered their ability to stem the flow of Albanian-peddled heroin into America.

By that time the NATO bombing of Serbia was in full swing, however, and the terrorists were, once again, American "allies."

The rest, as they say, is history.

AN AFTERTHOUGHT ON HISTORY

# A War For Human Rights?

*Frances Maria Peacock[1]*

In 1999 NATO attacked Yugoslavia, supposedly to prevent a "humanitarian disaster." It acted without a resolution from the UN Security Council, thus setting a precedent that a military action could be launched without a UN mandate. This action has had far-reaching consequences for international law and the United Nations, from Iraq to Georgia.

Separatist ambitions were being harbored in Kosovo as far back as the 1960s. They were reflected in demonstrations by Albanian activists in 1968 and further major unrest in 1981, a year after Tito's death.

When elected President of Serbia in 1989, Milosevic took steps to reduce the autonomy Kosovo had been given under the 1974 Constitution in an attempt to clamp down on Albanian unrest. This fuelled inter-ethnic tension: in July 1990 Albanian members of the Kosovo provincial assembly declared the province independent of the Republic of Serbia. Belgrade responded by suspending the Kosovo government and the parliament and placing tight restrictions on Albanian political activity. Two months later, in September, a second set of constitutional changes were introduced which further deprived Kosovo of its autonomy along with Vojvodina.

Prior to Rambouillet the Yugoslav government had offered an opportunity of substantial self-government for Kosovo, but nothing but total independence would suf-

---

1 Frances Maria Peacock is a political analyst based in Britain and author of numerous published papers on the conflict in the former Yugoslavia.

fice for the Albanian leadership. It seems likely that the conflict would have arisen even if the autonomy had been left in place because it was rooted in Albanian separatism, rather than Serbian intransigence. Leaked NATO documents appear to confirm this.

Sporadic attacks on Serbian targets began with the formation of the KLA in 1996. By February 1998 a low-intensity armed conflict between the KLA and Serbian forces was under way. As inevitably happens in such conflicts, innocent civilians on both sides also became victims. A fragile subsequent ceasefire was brought to an end by the Racak incident in January 1999. It prompted then-US Secretary of State, Madeleine Albright, to decide that something should now be done to protect the Albanians against Serb brutality, and prevent a "humanitarian disaster."

Racak was the trigger for the bombing campaign against Yugoslavia. It was preceded by the sham "negotiations" at Chateau Rambouillet. To the outside world it was made to look as if an effort was being made to resolve the conflict peacefully. In reality, the decision to bomb Yugoslavia had already been made several months earlier, well before Racak.

On March 15, 1999, when it was certain that the Serbs had rejected it, the Albanians signed the Rambouillet Accord. The US Secretary of State, who had been responsible for drawing up that remarkable document, "intentionally set the bar too high for the Serbs to comply," because "they need some bombing and that is what they are going to get." The Serbian side had never had any chance to resolve the crisis peacefully.

Several parallels can be drawn between the negotiations at Rambouillet and the talks held in Vienna in 2006 to resolve the issue of Kosovo's status. Both processes were characterized by media manipulation and disinformation, bias in favor of Albanians, pre-determined decisions, and most importantly, utter disregard for international law. There was never an intention in either case to reach a genuine agreement. Both sets of "negotiations" were staged to give the impression to the outside world that a real attempt was being made to resolve the issue peacefully.

Whatever the real reason for this war, it was not about human rights. Racak was not the "final straw" but a stage-managed trigger. KLA attacks against Serbs and loyal Albanians were ignored. Far worse transgressions by unsavory friends (Saddam before 1990) and even NATO allies (Turkey) had been blithely disregarded or minimized.

*Cui bono?* Kosovo is now home to a major U.S. military base, Camp Bondsteel. This has been strategically placed to give the United States a foothold in the Balkans, and is geographically crucial in relation to the Greater Middle East. The intervention in Kosovo has enabled the United States to transform NATO into a pliable tool of

Washington's policies thousands of miles outside its original zone. The outcome of the war fatally weakened Slobodan Milosevic internally and contributed to his fall.

History has reported itself several times since 1999, most notably in 2003 when military action was taken against Iraq without a UN mandate, and again in 2008 when Kosovo unilaterally declared itself independent in violation of international law. That Kosovo is anythong but *sui generis*, "unique case," was on display in the Caucasus in August 2008. It is only a matter of time before further eruptions of separatism are seen in other parts of the world where such ambitions are harbored.

# APPENDIX II

# Kosovo and the American Century

Thomas Fleming[1]

Let us be clear: this so-called war was not about human rights or ethnic cleansing. This NATO war was an act of criminal aggression against a small nation, the latest chapter in a history of American imperialism that began in Cuba and the Philippines one hundred years ago.

But what is the significance of Kosovo? The clue lies in the meaning of Kosovo for the Serbs. It is the land where the Serbian nation was forged in defeat. It was after the battle of Kosovo – over 600 years ago – that Serbs dedicated themselves to God, and it is in Kosovo, where their greatest churches are located. In taking Kosovo from the Serbs we are robbing them of their history and their identity, we are committing a kind of cultural genocide against their nation and that is the point.

In the new world order of the NATO empire there will be no nations, no religions, no cultures – just one vast free-trade global marketplace of producers and consumers. In destroying Kosovo we are destroying the Serbs, but we are also destroying ourselves. The bombing may have stopped, and NATO's empire of half a billion people has crushed ten million Serbs; but the real task for Americans has just begun: We can no longer expect the Serbs to fight for our freedom. Most Americans have always

1 Published immediately following the end of the hostilities, in June 1999, as Dr. Fleming's *Foreword* to *The Kosovo Dossier* (The Lord Byron Foundation, 1999). Thomas Fleming is President of The Rockford Institute and Editor of *Chronicles: A Magazine of American Culture*.

been, in their hearts, opposed to imperialism, even when presented in the benevolent rhetoric of proponents of "the American century." Henry Luce coined the phrase "the American Century" and gave it currency as an expression of the militant economic globalism that has characterized U.S. policy from the days of McKinley. Luce – the publisher of *Time* and *Fortune* – was the child of missionaries in China; a product, in other words, of American religious and cultural globalism. It is no small irony that this preacher's kid was the chief spokesman for a global movement that in its mature face has emerged as the principal enemy of the Christian faith.

The approach to Christianity taken by the post-modern post-civilized and post-Christian American regime is a seamless garment. At home, the Federal government bands prayer in school, enforces multiculturalism in the universities and encourages the immigration of non-Christian religious minorities that begin agitating against Christian symbols the day arrive. Abroad, the regime refuses to defend Christians from the genocide inflicted by Muslims in the Sudan, and in the Balkans it has waged a ruthless and inhumane war against the Serbs of the Krajina (currently in Croatia), Bosnia, Kosovo, and inner Serbia. The inhumanity of NATO's campaign against towns and villages, heating plants, television station, reveals – even in the absence of other evidence – the anti-Christian hatred that animates the Washington regime. The destruction of Christianity in the Balkans, from this perspective, is only the first step toward the eventual goal, which Volataire summarized in his phrase *écraser l'infame*, or rub out the infamy that is Christianity.

Luce was a big-business Republican who spoke the messianic language of progress and democracy, and after World War II, his magazines reinvented an America that was strangely detached from the realities of American life. His vision of America as one vast YMCA youth camp--albeit with nuclear weapons--was about as realistic as the images projected by his contemporary and rival, Walt Disney. Tailoring his message to patterns laid down by his country's political leaders, Luce did not believe that objective reporting was possible, much less desirable.

Today, Luce's successors in the media play the same game on a vastly bigger stage, and corporate America has merged the visions of Time-Warner-NBC and Disney-CNN-ABC into a global Ministry of Truth, whose only rivals are the equally sinister Rupert Murdoch, and the publishing-entertainment giants like Gulf-Western/ Simon & Schuster.

Luce did not invent the American Empire; he only shilled for it. His American Century began in the Philippines 100 years ago, when the American regime refined on the policies and techniques that were discovered in the Civil War that had ended less than 35 years previously. For a hundred years, American globalists have pursued their aims, checked occasionally by the will of ordinary people who, until recently, could not be fooled all of the time. William Appleman Williams, who devoted his life to what he called The Tragedy of American Diplomacy, detected three strains of American imperialism. His three approaches - commercial, military and progressive - are a useful starting point. The first of the three is the commercial expansion advocated by Republicans - McKinley, Taft, Hoover, and even Eisenhower, uneasy as he was about military-industrial complex.

Although all of these free-traders were occasionally willing to back up the politics of self-interest with gunboats, they preferred to rely, whenever possible, on dollar diplomacy. They were fairly frank about America's imperial role, which enabled them to be more cautious and more prudent than Democratic zealots like Wilson and the two Roosevelts. Their in age is that of America as banker and salesman to the world. Free Trade could be the route to market penetration, and one of the early slogans of commercial imperialists was the open door. Unfortunately, sometimes, the door had to be kicked in by the marines. As one spokesman for American industry put it a hundred years ago, One way of opening up a market is to conquer it. This is what Bill Clinton meant, when he justified his attack on Yugoslavia on the grounds that we needed a stable Europe as a market for American goods.

The second strain is represented by the military imperialists: two Roosevelts, the neoconservative hawks like Jean Kirkpatrick, by Bomber Clinton and his secretary of State, the Butcher of the Balkans. First put their trust in the navy (Mahan) and gradually switched to advocating reliance on air power: the common thread is a concern with long-range "projection of power" and a desire to minimize risks to our troops. The image is America as Cop or, increasingly, America as mercenary rent-a-cops hiring out to Saudi Arabia or Kuwait. Sometimes it is necessary to switch gears, from the democratic right to secede to preserving sovereignty. Considering how quickly the media switched principles on secession in the Balkans - yes to Croatia and Bosnia, no to the Bosnian and Krajina Serbs, yes to the Kosovo Albanians - it should not be much of a stretch, either for the journalists or their readers.

The third... Sentimental Imperialists, exemplified by Woodrow Wilson and Jimmy Carter, sugar-coated America's global mission with the language of democracy, progress, human rights. This approach justifies even more dangerous adventurism than the rent-a-cop militarism of George Bush. It is now, apparently, DOD policy to use the American military to reconstruct other countries on American model; America as social worker to the world.

Even the most tough-minded Americans are suckers for a messianic appeal. This has something to do with the Puritan legacy. McKinley, in declaring war on the people of the Philippines, a war that would cost the lives of more than 200,000 civilians, proclaimed the aim of our military administration was "to win the confidence, respect, and affection of the inhabitants... by assuring them... that full measure of individual rights and liberties which is the heritage of a free people, and by proving to them that the mission of the United States is one of benevolent assimilation."

In even more unctuous tones, Bill Clinton insists that he is not making war on the Serbian people but only on Slobodan Milosevic. Milosevic is still alive - so for that matter is Saddam Hussein - but hundreds of Serb civilians are dead and thousands injured. When our missiles hit the homes of peasants and kill a dozen civilians, we say it is an unfortunate accident or that the Serbs blew up their own houses. When Bill Clinton tells the world that "this is about our values," I wonder what values he means. The slaughter of the innocent? An addiction to lying? Perjury? Adultery? Treason? Rape?

There is, of course, a convergence of interests in these three strains. Bringing human rights to China means exporting pop commercial culture which degrades their peasantry to the level of ours and forces them into the global marketplace of jeans and cokes and McDonalds, while the militarists get to sell the most sensitive technology - or give it away in return for bribes - which thus alarms the right-wing paranoids in Middle America and gets them ready for all-out war, if necessary, with China.

American imperialism did not begin overnight and its progress is not the result of a cynical conspiracy. It was inevitable that European settlers would conquer the continent and perhaps tragically fated that they would then apply the lessons they had learned to the rest of the world. The three formative experiences were the Civil War, the Indian Wars, and above all the Spanish American War, and the techniques of manipulation and propaganda used in those conflicts are being applied--to the nth degree—in the NATO attack on Yugoslavia.

## 1. Demonization of one side and sentimentalization of victims

In the American Civil War, the dichotomy was: masters and slaves, and the Government in Washington was able to sell a war of conquest as a crusade for liberation. In the Spanish-American War the first dichotomy was evil Spaniards and virtuous natives, but then when in the Philippines the natives wanted to liberate themselves and establish their own government, another metaphor was adopted, this one from Indian Wars: hostiles and friendlies. The press worked overtime railing against the primitive culture and savage behavior of the natives - usually described as "niggers" by the soldiers. One soldier wrote home that his unit was ordered "to burn the town and kill every native in sight.... About 1,000 men, women, and native children were reported killed." he said, adding, "I am in my glory when I can sight my gun on some dark skin and pull the trigger." General Howling Jake Smith ordered his men to kill anyone who resisted—including women and children—along with all combatants, whom he defined as any male of 10 years or more. He got his nickname when he told his officers to turn an entire island into a howling wilderness.

Theodore Roosevelt, the Nobel Peace Prize laureate, never saw a war he didn't like, but constantly larded his rhetoric with references to the noble purpose of the Anglo-Saxon races in civilizing the benighted black and brown and yellow savages of the world. We used to be openly racist in our policy; now we are content to be ethnocentric, assuming that everyone would be an American if only he had a chance. Our posture toward the world is that of the stage Englishman who, when the frogs and dagos don't understand him, simply raises his voice. When Bill Clinton - who speaks no civilized language, including standard English - can't make himself understood, he speaks very loudly indeed, with bombs and missiles.

### 2. A symbolic incident

The Mexican War gave us a real massacre at the Alamo, but ever since we have found a series of phony incidents. The firing on Fort Sumter (which Lincoln eventually confessed was a set-up); the Gulf of Tonkin incident which never took place; The Battleship Maine, which the Spaniards did not blow up in Havana Harbor, is the perfect parallel to the media-created massacres in Sarajevo and the village of Racak in Kosovo. Every night on NATO TV we were shown hour after hour of footage of weary Albanian refugees and a few minutes - if that - of the people killed by the bombing. In the world of Disney-CNN, real atrocities are buried under layer after of faked incidents and commercial sentimentalism.

### 3. The media

As W.R. Hearst cabled his reporter in Cuba, when he said he could find no war going on, "You furnish the pictures; I'll furnish the war." Every petty conflict mobilizes the press and the intellectual classes in a progressive struggle against fascism, inhumanity, and an unending series of Hitlers and "holocausts."

Anyone who has studied the examples of the Roman, and British empires will find the rhetoric familiar. Julius Caesar plundered his way across Gaul, always on the pretext that he was defending Rome's Gallic allies, first from the Germans and then from each other. A century and a half later, Tacitus, who was himself a member of the

Roman imperial aristocracy, puts this summation of Roman policy in the mouth of a British rebel: "They make a desert and they call it peace." With the advantages of a classical education, America's British allies dubbed the NATO initial 1998 plan for Kosovo Operation Agricola in honor of the Roman general whose conquest of Britain had inspired his son-in-law Tacitus's characterization of the Roman Empire.

None of this would be possible without the eager complicity of the press, which has been conscripted into military service. This cozy relationship between government and the press is symbolized by the marriage of Jamie Rubin and Christiane Amanpour... [One of my favorites is the CNN "live" report with Amanpour who claimed to be showing live pictures Serbs violating an 8:00 PM cease-fire, but unfortunately the skies over Albania and Kosovo were blue and sunny at 3:20 AM. The footage had obviously been taken before the cease-fire.] Usually, the propaganda is on bigger scale, as when NATO officials warned Slobodan Milosevic – described as the "Serb leader" – against invading Montenegro, the very same language that Bob Dole (the Senator from Tirana, as he is called) when threatening the Serbs against restoring order in Kosovo.

## 4. National unity

During every conflict, with only the partial exception of Vietnam, we Americans have been told that we must support our boys. Pattern was set in Spanish-American War, when ex-confederates joined with their former enemies to defeat the Spanish empire and construct one of our own. Ever since we have exported our own conflicts to foreign shores in an unsuccessful effort to reconcile the warring races, regions, and religions of our continental US.

In the Kosovo conflict, whose purpose has never been defined (or rather defined once too often) Senator John McCain - who think he can climb to the White House on the bodies of dead Serb civilians - is saying, in essence, that we don't know why we are bombing Yugoslavia, but now that we are, we must send in ground troops to maintain the credibility of NATO. Even critics of the Clinton-Blair bombing reiterated their "support for the commander-in chief." That phrase will someday be viewed as the English translation of *We were only following orders*.

There is nothing new under the 3am sun, either in the theory or the practice of globalism. A century ago, when Uncle Sam was taking the Philippines, John Bull was mopping up the Boers. Winston Churchill advised the American cousins to be as ruthless in pursuit of their empire as the English were in South Africa. Like TR, Mr. Churchill – and, later, Sir Winston - was a rugged imperialist who believed in the joint destiny of Anglo-Saxon race in Britain and America. But the Boer War was actually beginning of end for British Empire - as many patriotic Englishmen like Chesterton recoiled in horror from ʳhe brutality of imperial conquest.

America did not learn its lesson in Philippines, or later in Vietnam. Badly checked in Southeast Asia, we believed we had learned the lessons of Vietnam--which is to leave complex and inscrutable foreign conflicts to the locals. In the 1980's, however, a new exuberance began to manifest itself, in Central America, for example, where shadowy agents of the Administration and the CIA played war-games that cost the lives of thousands of Nicaraguans and Salvadorans. When our allies murdered several leftist American priests, a sinister American diplomat named William Walker covered up the evidence and helped prepared the official lie given to the American people. It was that same William Walker who conveniently discovered the Racak massacre of 45 Albanian civilians and gave Bill Clinton his excuse for a war. That massacre, as it happens, never took place, according to an AP TV crew and a couple of seasoned French correspondents present at the scene, and to subsequent findings of foreign forensic pathologists.

It may be too late to go back to the wholesome policy of isolation, but if we must have global commercial hegemony, let us be honest about what we are doing and understand the limits. If we cannot go back to the days of Washington and Adams, let us at least recover the pragmatism of Hoover and Eisenhower. The global good intentions of Wilson pave the road to hell. The duplicity and incompetence of Mr. Clinton and his English poodle have succeeded only in awakening the Russian bear from his hibernation. As Byelarus and the Ukraine consider reintroducing nuclear weapons, Russia is considering an alliance with China and India against NATO. Between them the three countries account for more than one half of all humanity; so much for America's claim to the mystical "leadership of the international community."

So far from this period being the end of history, Bill Clinton has given us round two of the Cold War. This time around, however, the Russians know better than to believe all our malarkey about free markets and democratic human rights, and this time round the future of America in that conflict may be the proverbial snowball's chance in hell.

# APPENDIX III

# Afterword to
# The Kosovo Dossier (1999)

*Michael Stenton*[1]

There will be readers of this book who have long assumed, as a matter of course, that sooner or later America would use force on behalf of the Kosovo Albanians. Others will have been very puzzled as the Kosovo story grew and grew in 1998. Some readers may regard NATO's attack on Serbia as a moral necessity and others believe that the 'West' has gone mad and become mortally dangerous to the rest of the world. These views are so different that there is likely to be a parting of the ways, a great moral-political separation. Perhaps the West and the Rest will simply not converse for the next generation.

If anyone is genuinely interested in Kosovan autonomy – as something other than a prelude to Greater Albania - they would need a post-Milosevic strategy. A UN protectorate is not a policy, it is a legal wrapper. There cannot be autonomy unless it is negotiated, and the two sides have been refusing to negotiate for a very long time. Hence there will be no autonomy. There will be partition for Serbia or defeat for the KLA. Neither invading Kosovo nor bombing Belgrade can ever make true negotiations - dead since 1989 – finally happen. The bombing war cannot achieve the settlement

1 Published immediately following the end of the hostilities, in June 1999, as Dr. Stenton's *Afterword* to *The Kosovo Dossier* (The Lord Byron Foundation, 1999). Michael Stenton is the former Director of Studies of The Lord Byron Foundation.

that did not happen at Rambouillet, and it cannot bring back opportunities which were deliberately thrown away.

The immediate reason for the NATO war on Serbia is the US attempt to dictate a Kosovo settlement rather than facilitate a negotiation. Washington has ignored the lesson of Dayton, where international agreement about principles preceded a real negotiation about details, or rather it substitutes the myth of Dayton - US bombs solved the problem - f.  the truth. More broadly we can see an American wish to assert political and military leadership for the sake of doing so. Yugoslavia - since 1991 - has provided the excuse for redefining NATO's 'out of area' mission. The Americans have been making threats constantly since 1991. There may be - though this is probably still in the balance - an even worse motive in some minds: to push Russia back into a hostile posture and restart the arms race.

The point about these explanations of NATO action is that they are not 'causes' in competition with each other. They constitute a continuum of ambition along which the daily intentions of powerful people can advance and recede. The foreign policy community in Washington has been anti-Serb for some time, that is, they have chosen to live a mental world where the briefing and historical understanding of Balkan events comes ultimately from Bosnian Muslim and Albanian sources. The perspective is not, of course, Islamic, but it is built upon a secularized Muslim view of the Serbian problem. In 1994 this writer was told, by an official inside the State Department, that 'there are two sorts of people in this building: anti-Serbs and violent anti-Serbs'. This animus and this understanding would have been of limited consequence if the only issue was Serbia. But the Serbian question moved onto the global stage as it became evident that anti-Serbian intervention - the Janissary option - would make possible a dramatic shift in US policy on NATO and NATO expansion which would otherwise have been very difficult.

This is provides an answer to the question 'Why Kosovo?' The USA has been threatening the Yugoslav Army since 1991, but the earlier threats were premature and US policy was uncertain. What launched Washington ambition into higher orbit was the transformation of Bosnia and Herzegovina - and the Republic of Srpska in particular - into a NATO protectorate. This seemed to show that high-handedness in the name of political virtue could be made to work. But in so far as it did work – for instance by excluding Radovan Karadzic's party from power – it was based on aspects of the fine print of Dayton which have been pushed harder and further than anyone predicted in 1995.

NATO and the High Representative have claimed the authority to go anywhere, do anything, dismiss anyone from office, close down any TV station and even censor school books. American negotiators were carried away by their success in pushing the Bosnian Serbs from one concession to another. The whole experience of occupying Bosnia provided a template for the Kosovo intervention. Washington calculated that Milosevic had no serious alternative but to sign the same sort of treaty, a treaty which would give America - through various institutional interfaces - carte blanche to govern Kosovo as though it were a colony.

American strategy in the Republic of Srpska was, of course, noticed in Belgrade. At Rambouillet the Serbs found that their worst fears justified. Not only would real Yugoslav authority in Kosovo vanish beyond recall but Yugoslavia itself would be subject to NATO's military control. At very least this would completely erase any feeble consolation Belgrade might derive from the interim acceptance that Kosovo remained - in empty form - part of Yugoslavia. If the RS precedents held good, Serbia itself would be occupied after a succession of little crises and legal maneuvers. Many people believed before Rambouillet that Milosevic would, before or after a little bombing, sign up for Kosovan autonomy, but few would have thought so after reading the plan carefully and considering the amazing military protocol. American strategy was always based on getting Milosevic's compliance, but by 1999 there was some determination that there would be bombing first and compliance afterwards.

Shortly before the Kosovo War started, NATO expanded its membership to receive Hungary, Poland and the Czech Republic, and promises were made to the Baltic States. Shortly afterwards encouragement was offered to Romania and Bulgaria and the core military doctrine was changed at the Washington conference. We are today confronted with a potent but frightening fait accompli: a redefined NATO with a almost global remit to do humanitarian military interventions wherever Washington pleases and a chorus of commentators crying 'Nato cannot afford to lose'. Radical legal redefinitions are suddenly flashing up all over the screen. The left-liberal governments of Germany, Britain and France have allowed a sort of American coup d'etat against the NATO charter and the UN charter. And everyone saw this one coming a mile off.

The immediate, almost petty objection to NATO asserting a humanitarian mission in Kosovo is that America is the patron of the KLA. The Serbs are quite right about this. HMG knows it, the French and Italians know it and so do the Russians; though NATO had to pretend, at first, not to know. The French and Italian governments dare not complain, just as the French and British dared not complain during the UNPROFOR period in Bosnia when the Americans broke UN sanctions by delivering arms while pretending to be about to do so. Newspapers and TV companies, without a political signal, did not make the large investigative investment necessary to check out the KLA story and follow the heroin trail.

Another, more difficult matter, is the ideological pretext for intervention. During the Bosnian war and now again in Kosovo we are told, or more exactly we are made to feel we are being told, that a genocide was taking place; and we were told a little more plainly that ethnic cleansing was a sort of racial persecution and the idea 'Nazi' was invoked through the much repeated reference to horrors worse than anything seen since the second world war. The prevention of genocide must be an extremely powerful justification for armed action. But it is worth mentioning the record. The USA was consumed with indignation when the Indian Army stopped genocide in Bangladesh and when the Vietnamese Army topple Pol Pot. There were only threats of sanctions.

What is happening in Kosovo remains to be established; but for Bosnia it is simply not apparent that a genocide did take place. The casulaties were, at every stage, much exaggerated. Politicians still repeat the old Muslim claim that 250,000 people were killed in Bosnia. But there is simply no evidence for this figure. I believe the true figure is almost certain to be lower than 100,000 and could be as low as 50,000; it is probable that most died in battle and quite clear that the casualties were not at all overwhelmingly Muslim.

There was murder in Bosnia, sometimes mass murder, but there is no evidence of genocide in the normal meaning of that word. (The extensive definitions included in the Convention on Genocide, may mean that anyone knocking down mosques is guilty of genocide; there are certainly guilty Serbs on this count.) Ethnic cleansing is a charge that cannot be contested. But taking Bosnia and Croatia together, the Serbs ended up as much sinned against as sinning. Popular initiative and sinister instructions from Belgrade, Sarajevo and Zagreb have yet to be disentangled. The Serbs claim that they did not start it, but in 1991-92 Belgrade had most of the advantages and presumably carry the largest burden of responsibility.

But the motive was not racial, as Westerners assume all too easily. (If West Indians or Arabs were pushed out of London or Paris the motives would assuredly be racial.) But among Serbs, Croats and Muslims communal malice is not really racial - even less so than, say, in Northern Ireland where at least the ghost of a Celt/Saxon distinction lingers. Where ethnic cleansing was local it was an act of bitterness and revenge.

'We do not want to live with them!' was an accusation of treachery made by Serbs against those who had betrayed Yugoslavia out of nationalist malice. The punishment was to be sent to live in another part of the same small country. ('If you can't stand Yugoslavia because of the Serbs; why should Serbs take this Croatia or Bosnia of yours.') The Serbs were also aware that the Croats and Muslims were quietly confident that independence for their countries would accelerate a voluntary emigration of Serbs.

Even where ethnic cleansing was controlled and strategic this idea of punishment or retaliation was still effective. But there was also a sort national deterrence theory on offer: if you do 'x' we will punish your people 'y'. It had nothing much to do with the racial dreams and demons which drove the fascists of the forties. What the Serbs did in Croatia in 1991 and in Bosnia in 1992 was a brutal retort to the declarations of independence. But it was also a less bloody alternative to fighting a winner-takes-all war on indisputably Croat or Muslim territory. It was the improvisation of a crazed Yugoslav who could only retain power by plugging into Serbian nationalism but who never stopped believing that his opponents were Yugoslavs who would somehow wish to settle pragmatically.

If the Serbs had levelled Zagreb to the ground 'to save Yugoslavia' the West might have understood, but the milder policy of ethnic cleansing was extremely visual, it seemed exceptionally cruel and neo-nazi although it was far from being the most violent option. True, some atrocities were committed by Serbian fascists; but they did not control state policy or define Serbian hopes, and their Croat and Muslims cousins behaved just as badly. Once the neo-Nazi hypothesis was launched, everything that happened was additional evidence. Hence, the bombardment of Sarajevo (1992) was an outrage, but the bombardment of Belgrade (1999) can become a duty that strains few consciences.

Since it is the perceived ideological context for human suffering that arouses the strongest feeling, it is worth saying that Milosevic is no more a racist than was Stalin or Suleiman the Magnificent. His ethno-terrorism has not received convincing interpretation. It is not compulsive but yet it seems to fascinate him. It obtains a short-term kick of gutter nationalist enthusiasm, it covers Serbian patriotism with shame but it is above all a signal to the powerful that it is time to make crude bargains with 'the Man' in Belgrade.

All these three qualities appeal to him. Ethnic cleansing is not Milosevic's redneck solution to the Kosovo problem – he knows that the Albanian civilians will probably go home in the end - it is the tool of a clever, cruel but often foolish man with a perverse understanding of political reality. It is intimidation plus a declaration of power and authority: Ottoman and Bolshevik in the worse sense of those words. His foolishness, and parochialism, has lain in demanding to be understood as the Yugoslav that he is; his perversity is his reasoned but wrong estimate that being cruel to civilians can force his opponents and enemies to act responsibly.

Milosevic is often described as a man who does tactics not strategy. The judgment assumes, unreliably, that his goals would be nationalist if he were strategic about them. But he did, it seems, make a huge strategic choice. He decided to accept what he once worked so hard to avoid - war in Serbia. This decision was, it now seems clear, already made when he dismissed Jovica Stanisic, his security chief, immediately after the Holbrooke agreement in October 1998. Kosovo was slowly pushed into disaster when America started pawing at it. Military intervention in Kosovo was not remotely a regional requirement before 1998. Unfortunately, European governments reacted to American pressure in a direct, separate and not a collective way. Europe was curiously passive judged against the previous diplomatic inclination to leave the Balkans to settle down. But the European public is not really very different; educated Europeans and educated Americans seem to have an identical impatience with Balkan quarrels and a identical willingness to drop bombs on problems.

Clinton is not a bomber because he is gazing at opinion polls. He is a bomber because bombing is what America does best. American bombing must be made to work - somewhere, someday - if CNN-led military utopianism is to be globally intimidating. The future will have arrived only when America is truly equipped to win a war by remote-control. The military experiment which beckons to his advisers more than the predicament of civilians whose position it has made at least an order of magnitude worse than before. If air power fails yet again they are more likely to demand escalation than to settle. Senator McCain has already thrust himself to the forefront of Republican contenders for the presidency by demanding a 'real' war, a new American doctrine ('rogue state rollback') and a warning that the EU cannot have a 'defense identity' other than NATO.

If NATO were going to attempt to make a civilized demonstration of force, there would have been a build-up of NATO divisions in Croatia and Hungary with the capture of Belgrade as the military goal: there would have been a Free Serbia committee and a declaration in advance to partition or, less plausibly, limited autonomy, and an initial demand or resignation of the President and fresh elections. This would have been no less illegal, but, after a promise to the UN of withdrawal in nine months, it might have won grudging Russian tolerance. But the Class of '68 have decided on high-tech massacre not a war with a useful outcome. The empty minds have grown sinister. They know that in the long term, infantry is the Achilles heel of NATO.

Imperialist high-mindedness is back but in a genuinely new form. Christian religion, national flags and national rivalry will play little or no part. But the Western yearning for excitement and importance which took the British to Peking, Kabul and Khartoum, the French to Fashoda and Saigon and the Americans to Manila has now re-emerged not as the search for colonies to 'exploit' but as the search for places where the moral fiber and technical superiority of Western civilization can, once more, be demonstrated by all means including violence. America will conduct this process, sometimes for very specific strategic or economic reasons, but an expanded First World is already collectively engaged in one way or another.

The old imperialism flourished on the back of the enormous technical and cultural superiority of Europe to the rest of the world, and it shrank rapidly as the colonized world acquired European skills, science and military expertise. But perhaps European imperialism crumbled too quickly. Soviet and American hostility hastened its end. The British in particular were curiously unresisting, though they seemed determined to advertise their military skills in Kenya, Cyprus, Malaya and Arabia. The truth is that the end of imperialism was not what it seemed. It is possible that the natural decay of colonial rule - as seen in India - was artificially accelerated elsewhere leaving a sense in imperial heartlands that something wrong, unnecessary and premature had happened even among imperial servants whose commitment to self-government was perfectly genuine.

During the Cold War there was an absolute ideological requirement for 'the West' to abandon what remained of empire, because the fire in the Chinese Revolution was anti-imperial. But there was also a requirement for the use of post-imperial advantages. Iran, for instance, is the enemy of America today because of the ruthless Anglo-American pursuit of these advantages. But as the patriotism of the neo-imperial British middle-class went off-shore - in exactly the financial sense of that word - the second strongest economy in Europe went into a decline. The James Bond films represented the fantasies of British post-imperial families hoping to do well in an American world. Good old England was still a bit special, but one's hopes for the good life - fast, cosmopolitian, sybaritic, sexual and violent - depended on plugging into the larger host.

European neo-imperialism in the Cold War context was deflagged, stripped of symbolism, unified, globalized and made US-friendly. (France was the interesting, if hesitant exception.) But it was the passion that could not speak its name until Cold War neo-imperialism could be reflagged as globalism. This happened only at the very end of the century - between the Gulf War and Kosovo War. Post-colonial governments had been much less competent and far more grandiose than they should have been; then they became venal and often contemptible. Anti-colonialism lost its intellectual power well before it was pushed away as irrelevant. It had no explanation of post-colonial bungling except that the legacy of imperialism was still poisoning the former colonies. By the eighties it was an open secret in the European heartlands that decolonization had failed. The colonies needed strong patronage again, but the patrons had found a way of collecting such advantages as were worth having without the expense and military exposure of formal empire. In 1968 it had seemed that the swelling anti-imperial chorus in the General Assembly of the United Nations would stamp out neo-colonial bad practice, but the tide seemed to turn against the third world after 1973.

In the 1980s the British lived in reduced circumstances. They did not make their machine-tools any more but they did have GCHQ at Cheltenham and sold Harrier jump jets and fancy avionics, and could get Sidewinder missiles on a priority basis. During the Falkland war, some Germans grumbled enviously that they were not allowed do to that sort of thing any more, and the French elite were very sour and expressed considerable distaste for British jingoism. Now that is all behind us. The French have almost stopped (in public) sulking about American leadership, the Germans have been greeted as America's chief partner in Eastern Europe, and the British have no wish to fight solo ever again. We can all go to war together, when we feel good about it, and be equally engaged in the collective assertion of 'Western values'. We can even bomb TV stations in their name.

The fall of the Berlin wall was always likely sooner or later. What was less obvious, until 'Desert Storm' in Iraq, was how this would reinvigorate something to be called 'the West'. But not until the siege of Sarajevo was it clear just how strong the current would become. After 1989 everyone was invited to bid for a special relationship with the USA, and everyone wanted to bid. For the first time ever, the imperial terrain at America's feet matched and exceeded Britain's imperial sway a hundred years before. America's imperial potential was not lessened by the collapse of communism, it was enhanced.

America had also changed since the Vietnam era. Until the 1970s Washington seemed short of overseas expertise to a degree Europeans found exasperating. The Europeans still had the old men who knew best and they still had the right contacts. But by the 1990s, American universities were out-performing Europe in the production of second and third world specialists. Even more striking, the younger generation of aspirant politicians and bankers in the third world were likely to have been educated in those same American universities. American immigration policy turned out to have had - deliberately or not - a truly imperial value.

Modern America does not have the unchallenged economic hegemony of the Eisenhower years, but in 1998/99 it did not need European assistance to act or understand or to make policy. Indeed, America could project its understanding and policies onto Europe as the media market became more global. This, conversely, was more necessary than ever. The Europeans had to be persuaded not to use their real economic muscle to set up in opposition to America in places like the Balkans. Most Americans might still have little interest in distant parts, but the same had been true of most Englishman in 1900. The US foreign policy establishment has to work out just how far that matters and how much it does not. But they usually get their way.

Imperialism, as Kipling knew and as Victor Kiernan repeated and as Edward Said reminds us, is a cultural force. Said's leftism, his invocations of 'secular humanism' and his anxiety to make reading literature a contribution to universal liberation may seem tedious to the unsympathetic, but he is right to notice that the assumptions of imperialism did not disappear simply because racism went out of fashion and the colonies became independent. Culture continued to carry the existential marks of the imperial condition and opportunity can reignite imperial functionality however apparently buried and dormant. The pride of the English in their law, of the French in their lawyers and of the Germans in their *Ordnung* is very old - much older than that brief moment of hubris called 'scientific racism' - and America has inherited all three. America's own contribution has been to perfect the repudiation of racism and sexism and make it the centerpiece of the Euro-American message. CNN provides the most intensely ideological images since the Nazi newsreels. The benign ethos of globalism is endlessly displayed as multi-racial kitsch. The skepticism of the anti-racialists of yesteryear is neutralised by the utopian selflessness of modern marketing.

Cultural imperialism was seductive, compelling for its host and culturally intimidating. Victims and opponents were invited to contemplate the strength of a dominant culture and despair. What has changed is that we call it 'global'. The experience in the Balkans today is of resourcelessness. One must plug into the West - its power centers and its culture - and pray for favor and try to be noticed in the right way. Hence the readiness of Balkan countries to damage themselves to help America damage Serbia. Looking for favor is the only game in town. If only it were just the money! Imperial culture - today one says global culture - confiscates respect for what is local and native and replaces it with something universal however bad. Africa yesterday, the Balkans today. A Macedonian Albanian announces that he prefers Coca-Cola to Cyrillic. It is at exactly this point that imperialism is recognizable as an appropriate name for what is on offer.

The intermittent moral absolutism of the West cannot be opposed by mere condemnation. Its one potent question - are we prepared to watch them die or starve or wallow in ignorance or criminality? - will not go away even if we know that feeding them or stopping their wars will rarely have the exact effect we would wish. Genuine dilemmas about our human responsibility for one another are there to reactivate the viral imperialism of the re-extended West. And every argument against imperial mission-creep is the siren song of the Devil. Arguments from complexity are not so much judged as felt theologically. If the war against the past is a just war, its justice is meant to be revealed in its pragmatic simplicity. But it is a war that will need lots of lies. In any case, the more arrogant the new doctrine, the greater the willingness to lie for the truth.

The spiritual niches in which communities once sheltered from mainstream influences are blown away as remorselessly as the rainforest is cut down. Whether we like it or not - a phrase most editorialists manage to employ in every pronouncement they make about the Kosovo war - everyone looks likely to end up inside a belief system defined by some sort of globally-viable ideology. The process is long past half-way.

And what is viable is partly intellectual and partly power politics. The power to authorize new lies is what the Orthodox always feared in Rome; the power to authorize new lies about law, and defend them with a censorship of fact, is what half the world fears about the West today. We can all chose some modern half-truth that serves the West against the Rest in the way the *filioque* served those aggressive Latins who pushed the Roman curia into a contest with the Greeks.

Can there be anti-imperial critical thought that is not a rehash of Marxism? The debate about liberation theology suggests this question has engaged Roman Catholic attention for some time, and it is quite possible that in the Orthodox world, as well as in Latin America, an expiring Marxism has donated something to Christian democratic politics. Mexico, South Africa, Iran and Israel all have serious reservations about the Kosovo aggression. These are special countries - theologically aware - which simply cannot be uncritical about the West. In Western Europe the greatest doubts are in Italy and Ireland.

The *Frankfurter Allgemeine* is very cross that the Pope disapproves of the Kosovo War. Why, the paper thundered, should we have studied carefully Catholic just war doctrine if it all goes out of the window the moment the old man gets cold feet? But why did the old man get cold feet? The Pope had no difficulty about being a militant friend of Croatia and Bosnia. However, he has now seen something he does not like, which others saw earlier. He has seen war for war's sake, war as the political demonstration of a vast ambition, war as the moral toy of the immensely rich who will refuse to pay for, or even think about, the damage they will do. The war in Iraq has taken place, is still taking place. The Pope disliked that too.

Unless there is an understanding of war so universal that it can act as a check on the powerful, we will not escape the universal death that we learnt to fear a generation ago. Clinton and Blair may imply that they will solve this problem by making a universal empire to abolish war. But they cannot deliver. The pretence is so empty and unreal that the idea has to be left work for itself to create a feeling that in a shrinking world, and with a lot of US R&D... The truth is, surely, that the children of the fifties and sixties did not live in fear; they were far too complacent, but they were saved by extremely serious minorities - both in power and opposition - who did their worrying for them. This old guard has now departed. The new generation of Western leaders feel the Bomb has gone away. They have dropped the showy moralism of their youth: it lost them votes and the electors seemed not to want to know. In any case, it is evident that the middle ground now wants them to be resolute.

Much of the lazy support for nuclear disarmament was linked to the pain and distress caused by having to think about nuclear weapons and nuclear theories. The present thought-pattern is perhaps as follows: nuclear deterrence was obscene and we wanted it to go away; but people did not want a purely moral position so we agreed to ignore the question completely. It has now gone away, as we always wanted, and we are not going to bring it back by taking deterrence seriously again. The feeling of the times is that since the USSR has gone, no one will play brinkmanship with NATO. But one regiment of the old guard that kept us safe was a part of the USSR. It may no longer be there, yet the bombs remain. Did not we, in our days of perceived conventional weakness, refuse to rule out first use of nuclear weapons?

The strategic risks of the war against Yugoslavia may be as small as NATO would like to believe. But the strategic question in Moscow has been transformed. It has become terribly simple - 'If not now, when?' Let us hope that the answer is 'later' and that the emphasis is still on conventional weapons. Eventually we may be told that the Kosovo war started because excited politicians overruled the planners and professionals. The planning took place during Clinton's impeachment, but the President could not have cancelled if he had wished. The decision to bomb Belgrade without a complete war plan suggests considerable confidence even if we judge it as incompetence. This confidence may, of course, have a pragmatic basis called 'Milosevic', but the confident rhetoric of the war seems to express a broader confidence that preceded it. After all, confidence in getting Euro-American public support has been, it seems, entirely justified. But the confidence that Russia cannot react does not come from the politicians.

The moral ballast provided by the Second World War generation is now too small to help. There is a large public - larger in Europe than America - sufficiently unfamiliar with war to'v. tempted by violent utopianism and insufficiently inquisitive to ask whether there is anything more to Kosovo than the propaganda barrage about atrocity. As in Bosnia, atrocity becomes the whole story. If we are not Christian we are still post-Christian and this means that we still can yearn for utopia where heaven stood, for a potent value where there was faith and transcendence. Society must in some way refer to a utopian goal, and so must leadership. A world justified without any utopian elements would be deeply uncomfortable. But there is a problem. Some forms of utopianism have been dumped: above all social equality. What is left is the pursuit of ever-widening self-realization, which is arguably utopian. But something more generous is required. As we withdraw from constructed utopianism we seem to find more causes which require strategies of rescue, of utopian intervention.

The idea that we want war because we want someone to take the pictures of suffering off the TV screen is too simple. We may guess that someone will take the pictures off, we may know that similar events often take place without pictures even being shot, but this does not matter. The world is big and wicked, but when we are invited to say thumbs down to bad people we do so because life and TV must include some moral dimension. Turning thumbs down is what we have time for, it is how we can do something. Everyone must have rights which indicate the way out of their suffering, including animals, and we can intervene to enforce those rights.

A post '68 generation whose idealism was always unstructured and was progressively compacted by the shrinking of Left convictions wants to rescue the suffering. The objection that intervention is a set-up, that there are better causes, that the facts do not fit the crusade, misses obvious points known to all viewers. TV is always selective, and not everyone (or every animal) can be helped; and it feels right to apply the Good Samaritan principle even if the TV selects which roads we tread. Manipulation does not matter if we are fundamentally confident that globalism is liberating and progressive.

To be capable of 'doing something' sustains moral self-respect, if we can suppress the thought that we are not so much moral actors as consumers of predigested choices. Intervention in foreign parts was, in the days of old empire, often imposed on reluctant politicians by newspaper campaigns against 'barbarism' inspired by a few militants. Not much has changed. Good, old-fashioned imperial hysterics have revived in the CNN era. America is now Everyman. Once there was a president who declared himself ein Berliner but said it in such wonderfully bad German that he clearly did not believe it. Today another president imaginatively supposes all suffering souls to be virtual Americans. This is an imperialist kitsch - 'the last, best hope of mankind' - to which, unfortunately, most educated Americans can respond. It is an imperial delusion.

A consent to war rooted in parliamentary debate would enable Europe to inform Washington that there is no room for Turkey in NATO while Turkish Kurdistan lacks the security and freedoms we hope to bestow on Albanians. But if consent is a demotic reaction to pictures the political contract can be extremely narrow. An impulse purchase is made and repeated until there is a pattern. There is almost no moral exertion in today's assent to NATO violence. The bangs and flashes of NATO bombs incinerating chemical plants, TV studios and power stations will, if sustained long enough, even more terrible for civilians than fifteen minutes to pack and a trek to the Albanian border. But the citizen-viewer wants to make a shopper's quick decision and is fed up of hearing excuses. There may be worse to come. It would be foolish to doubt that one element in the approval ratings of the war is the sheer pleasure of getting to see those wonderful glowing explosions.

We are living in a virtual Coliseum where exotic and nasty trouble-makers can be killed not by lions but by the magical machines of the Imperium. As the candidates for punishment – or martyrdom – are pushed into the arena we react to the show as imperial consumers, not as citizens with a parliamentary right to stop it.